DATE DUE

SALADIN

Sultan of Egypt and Syria

RICHARD WORTH

Enslow Publishers, Inc.
40 Industrial Road
Box 398
Berkeley Heights, NJ 07922
USA

http://www.enslow.com

Library of Congress Cataloging-in-Publication Data

Worth, Richard.
    Saladin : Sultan of Egypt and Syria / Richard Worth.
        p. cm. — (Rulers of the middle ages)
    Includes bibliographical references and index.
    ISBN-13: 978-0-7660-2712-1
    ISBN-10: 0-7660-2712-0
    1. Saladin, Sultan of Egypt and Syria, 1137–1193—Juvenile literature. 2. Egypt—Kings
and rulers—Biography—Juvenile literature. 3. Syria—Kings and rulers—Biography—
Juvenile literature. 4. Crusades—Juvenile literature. I. Title. II. Series.
    DS38.4.S2W67 2006
    956'.014092—dc22
    [B]

                                                                            2006011734

Printed in the United States of America

10 9 8 7 6 5 4 3 2 1

To Our Readers:
We have done our best to make sure all Internet Addresses in this book were active and
appropriate when we went to press. However, the author and the publisher have no control over
and assume no liability for the material available on those Internet sites or on other Web sites they
may link to. Any comments or suggestions can be sent by e-mail to comments@enslow.com or to
the address on the back cover.

Illustration Credits: © Corel Corporation, p. 27; Enslow Publishers, Inc., pp. 8, 65; Illustrated
by Michael Grimsdale, SaudiAramco.com, pp. 32, 73, 80; John Feeney, SaudiAramco.com, p. 42;
Original painting by Corey Wolfe, p. 6; © 2006 Jupiterimages Corporation, pp. 10, 132; Public
domain image from Wikipedia.org, pp. 15, 76; Reproduced from *Doré's Illustrations of the
Crusades* by Gustav Doré published by Dover Publications, Inc., pp. 12, 88, 99, 105, 112, 126,
136; SaudiAramco.com, pp. 19, 21, 56, 60;

Illustration Used in Design: Reproduced from Full-Color Picture Sourcebook of Historic
Ornament, published by Dover Publications, Inc.

Cover Illustration: Original painting by Corey Wolfe.

CONTENTS

THE CONQUEST OF JERUSALEM

IN SEPTEMBER 1187, SALADIN DREW UP A LARGE army of over twenty thousand soldiers in front of the walls of Jerusalem, one of the Western world's most celebrated cities. Jerusalem is sacred to Jews, who established a capital there around 1000 B.C. under King David. The city is also sacred to Christians. Jesus Christ was crucified in Jerusalem in A.D. 33. He was buried in the Holy Sepulcher there. Christians believe that he arose from the dead. Finally, Jerusalem is a holy city to Muslims. They believe that the founder of their religion, Muhammad, rose into heaven on the back of a winged horse. That horse had flown skyward from the location of the Dome of the Rock, which was a mosque built in Jerusalem in A.D. 692. (A mosque is a Muslim place of worship.)

In 638, Jerusalem was conquered by Muslim armies. They held it for more than three hundred years. It became part of a vast Muslim empire that stretched from present-day Afghanistan to Spain. But in 1099, an army of Christian

Crusaders from western Europe invaded Palestine, located along the Mediterranean Sea. The Crusaders conquered Jerusalem after a bloody siege. Once they occupied the city, Crusaders pillaged Jerusalem. They killed an estimated twenty thousand Muslims as well as a vast number of Jews living there. Jerusalem became the capital of a Christian kingdom, a Crusader state, located in the center of Palestine.

In the 1170s, a new Muslim leader appeared—Saladin. After wiping out the Crusader army in 1179 and conquering most of their cities, Saladin finally turned on Jerusalem in 1187. The city was defended by Balian of Ibelin. He was a brave knight who had fought against Saladin in the past. Balian had come to Jerusalem because he wanted to remove his wife from the city. He stopped at Saladin's camp outside the city. Balian asked Saladin's permission to complete his mission. Saladin said that Balian could enter Jerusalem and collect his wife, if they left on the following day.

Balian agreed. Once inside the city, however, he was asked by the inhabitants to take charge of its defense. Balian had given his word to Saladin to leave Jerusalem. Therefore, he went back and asked Saladin's permission to take over the city's defenses. Saladin agreed, realizing that Balian felt his religious beliefs required him to stay and defend Jerusalem. As historian Karen Armstrong wrote, "Both men believed in the same code of honor; both respected the sanctity of an oath."[1]

With ten thousand defenders, Balian hoped to hold back the Muslim army. He wanted to keep Jerusalem in the

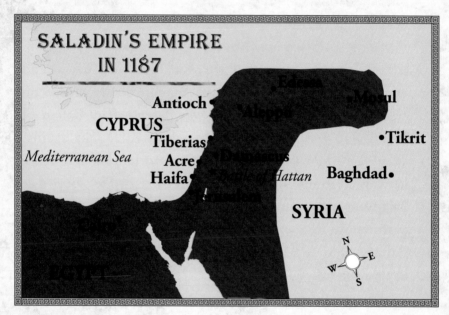

The kingdom of Jerusalem and Saladin's Empire in 1187 A.D.

hands of the Crusaders. However, the city was desperately short of food and water. The usual population of Jerusalem was thirty thousand. But the population had swelled to sixty thousand. Many Christians had fled to Jerusalem from the cities already conquered by Saladin.

Saladin's army, with its yellow banners flying, had advanced toward Jerusalem in late September. Along the way, the leading soldiers were ambushed by a small army of Christians. The Muslims lost many men. However, the Christian soldiers were eventually beaten back inside the gates of Jerusalem. Saladin finally encamped in front of Jerusalem's western walls and began his attack on September 26. Muslim sharpshooters shot their arrows at the defenders on the walls. According to one Christian, one "could not show a finger above the ramparts without being hit, so thick was the shower of Arabian [Muslim] arrows."[2]

The archers could only soften up the defenders on the walls. Arrows alone were not strong enough to break through the strong walls of Jerusalem. The attack against the western walls was not successful. So Saladin moved his army to the northern walls of the city. According to Ernoul, a thirteenth-century historian, Saladin set up his camp on the Mount of Olives, outside Jerusalem. This gave him a view inside Jerusalem.[3]

The Muslim leader sent for huge catapults. They were used to hurl giant boulders and large javelins against the northern walls of the city. Meanwhile, some of his soldiers dug tunnels beneath the walls. They supported these tunnels with wooden beams. Then they set the beams on

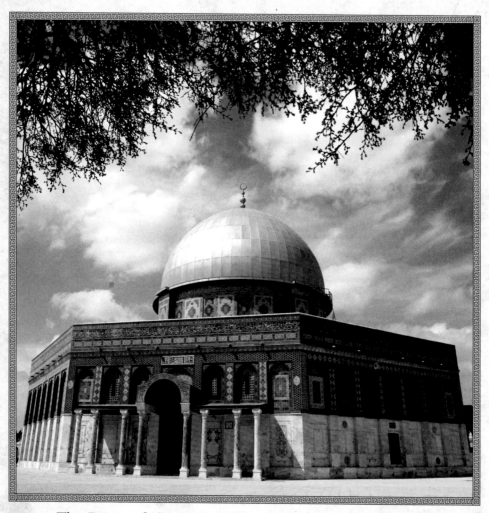

The Dome of the Rock (pictured as it looks today) is the building in Jerusalem most sacred to the Muslims.

fire, bringing down a large tower. This opened a way through the walls of the city and into Jerusalem.

The situation inside Jerusalem grew worse. Balian and the other leaders of Jerusalem met together to decide how to deal with it. Some of them wanted to continue fighting even if every soldier was wiped out. But Balian decided that the city should not try to hold out against Saladin. He was prepared to surrender the city. At first, Saladin was not inclined to treat the defenders of Jerusalem with any mercy. He remembered what had happened to the Muslims almost a century earlier. In addition, Saladin had taken an oath to avenge the deaths of so many Muslims in 1099.

But Balian told him:

> Know, O Sultan, that there are very many of us in this city, God alone knows how many. At the moment we are fighting half-heartedly in the hope of saving our lives, hoping to be spared by you as you have spared others; this is because of our horror of death and our love of life. But if we see that death is inevitable, then by God we shall kill our children and our wives, burn our possessions . . . come out to fight you like men fighting for their lives, when each man, before he falls dead, kills his equals; we shall die with honor, or win a noble victory!

Balian said that the Crusaders would fight to the last man and destroy the entire city.[4]

After consulting his advisors, Saladin decided to break his oath and spare the inhabitants of Jerusalem. They would be freed after paying a small amount of money, or ransom. This was a common practice in warfare during the

After Saladin captured Jerusalem, he still allowed Christian pilgrims to visit the Church of the Holy Sepulcher.

Middle Ages. On October 2, 1187, Saladin entered the holy city of Jerusalem. By his orders, most of the residents were not held captive by the conquering Muslims. They were ransomed. According to historian P. H. Newby, Saladin did not hold any poor elderly people who could not afford the ransom. "Saladin's generosity," Newby wrote, "was regarded not only by Muslims but by the . . . Christians as extraordinary."[5]

There was no killing or pillaging, as the Christians had done in 1099. Shortly after entering the city, Saladin moved into a small mosque—a Muslim holy place. This became his headquarters. He occupied a humble office, not a great palace. Saladin spared the Church of the Holy Sepulcher so Christians could continue to worship in the city. Christians were permitted to remain in the city and practice their religion. But they had to pay a tax to the Muslim government. Saladin also called back the Jews. They had been driven from Jerusalem during the Christian conquest.

The Dome of the Rock was a Muslim place of worship that had been converted to a church by the Crusaders. From his headquarters, Saladin ordered that the Christian church that had been built at the sacred Dome of the Rock should be taken down. In this way, the Muslim shrine could once again be visited by Muslim pilgrims. A cross was removed by Muslim soldiers from the top of the Dome of the Rock as well. "When they reached the top," wrote the Muslim historian Ibn al-Athir, "a great cry went up from the city and from outside the walls, the Muslims crying . . . in their joy, the [Crusaders] groaning in consternation and grief. So loud and piercing was their cry that the earth shook."[6]

In addition, Saladin decreed that the al-Aqsa Mosque, which the Christians had used as a stable, should be cleansed with rose water. Then the mosque could once again become the center of Muslim worship in Jerusalem. "The Koran was raised to the throne. . . . Prayer-mats were laid out and the religious ceremonies performed in their purity," wrote Muslim historian Imad al-Din.[7]

As historian James Reston, Jr. has written,

> By the exemplary behavior of his soldiers as they took charge of Jerusalem in 1187, Saladin did himself great credit as a wise leader. . . . By his protection of the Holy Sepulcher and the other Christian holy sites, his tolerance of other faiths would be long remembered. His actions seemed to define what it meant to be a good Muslim.[8]

This was the Age of Chivalry. Many leaders, both Christian and Muslim, believed strongly in values such as duty, honor, and courage. By his actions, Saladin earned a reputation as someone who exemplified these values.

Nevertheless, Christians in western Europe vowed to avenge the loss of Jerusalem. In 1187, they launched another crusade. This was aimed at taking back the Holy City from Saladin. Pope Gregory VIII called on knights across Europe. He urged them to carry out their duty to the Christian faith and begin a new crusade to the Holy Land. The Pope promised these knights "eternal life" in heaven "whether they shall survive or whether die. . . ." if the knights joined the Crusade.[9]

Saladin rex Aegypti

The original title of this fifteenth century image of Saladin reads "Saladin rex Aegypti," meaning "Saladin, king of Egypt."

In this crusade, Saladin would clash with the great Christian knights of Europe. The outcome increased Saladin's fame as a general. It also added to his reputation as a compassionate, chivalrous leader. Today, Saladin is still considered among the great heroes of the world. Indeed, he is highly respected by both Muslims and Christians.

SALADIN AND THE MUSLIM WORLD

SALADIN'S EARLY LIFE WAS SPENT IN SYRIA, THE heart of the Muslim empire. As he grew up, he was strongly influenced by his father and his uncle. Both men held important positions in the Muslim government.

Salah al-Din Yusuf, known as Saladin, was born about 1138 in Tikrit. This city is located on the Tigris River in present-day Iraq. Saladin's father, Najm al-Din Ayyub, was governor of the city. Saladin's family were Kurds, a large group of nomads who had settled in towns and cities located in Iraq, Armenia, and nearby areas. Ayyub and his brother Asad al-Din Shirkuh had been born near the town of Darwin. It was part of Armenia. Ayyub was a gifted political leader. Shirkuh—shorter and fatter than his brother—was a skilled military commander.

Shortly after Saladin was born, his father became governor of Baalbek. The city was southwest of Tikrit, in present-day Lebanon. Saladin was probably educated in the Baalbek Great Mosque. A mosque is a center of education and religious worship for Muslims—followers of Islam.

THE RELIGION OF ISLAM

The founder of Islam was Muhammad. He was born about A.D. 570 in Mecca, a town in present-day Saudi Arabia. The merchants of Mecca carried on a flourishing trade with Arab nomads who raised sheep and goats. The merchants also traded with Syria, Egypt, Palestine, and Persia. Among the traders who lived in Mecca was a widow named Khadija. Muhammad married her and together they had several children.

When he was forty, Muhammad experienced a vision in which he saw the angel Gabriel. The angel told Muhammad that he was a prophet of God, whom the Muslims call Allah. From that time on, Muhammad began preaching the words of God. He also tried to convert people in Mecca. Among Muhammad's first followers were his wife, Khadija, and their children. But the powerful people in Mecca began to persecute him and his followers. In 622, Muhammad finally left Mecca for another city, located northward, today known as Medina. The people there had invited him to come and lead them. This journey is called by Muslims the Hijra.

Here, Muhammad was welcomed by people who believed in his teachings. Medina became the center of Islam. Muhammad led his followers in battles against the people of Mecca. Eventually he returned to Mecca in 630,

Medina as it looks today

MUSLIM CALENDAR

The Muslim calendar begins in A.D. 622 with the Hijra of Muhammad. Therefore, the year 622 in the Christian calendar is the year one in the Muslim calendar. While a Christian year is 365 days, the Muslim year is about 354 days.

where the people had finally accepted his beliefs. Muhammad's teachings, considered the exact and direct words of God by his followers, were written down in a holy book. This book is called the Koran.

Saladin studied the teachings of the Koran during his education in Baalbek. He also learned the Five Pillars of Islam. Among them is that "there is no god but God, and Muhammad is the prophet of God." The second pillar requires Muslims to pray five times a day. According to the other pillars, Muslims are to give part of their money to charity; make a journey to Mecca, at least once; and, for one month of the Muslim calendar, not eat or drink from dawn until sunset.

EARLY MUSLIM CONQUESTS

Muhammad died in 632. He was succeeded as the leader of Islam by his son-in-law, Abu Bakr. He was called the *kaliph* or *caliph*, which means successor to Muhammad. Over the next century, Muslim caliphs led the Arab people who lived in the Middle East on the road of conquest. In 638, they conquered the ancient city of Jerusalem.

The Kaaba (center) is the holiest shrine of Islam. During the pilgrimage to Mecca, called the Hajj, Muslim pilgrims run and walk around the Kaaba seven times while praying.

Meanwhile, Muslim armies had conquered vast areas of the Middle East. They drove eastward into Afghanistan. They advanced westward through North Africa. In the eighth century, they conquered Spain. Muslim caliphs established a magnificent capital at Damascus, located in present-day Syria. Later, a group of Muslim leaders known as the Abbasids moved the capital to Baghdad, in present-day Iraq. Located along the Tigris and Euphrates rivers, Baghdad was selected as the capital by Caliph al-Mansur.

"This is the site on which I shall build," the caliph reportedly said. "Things can arrive here by way of the Euphrates, Tigris, and a network of canals. Only a place like this will support the army and the general populace."[1] The area around the rivers was a fertile land for growing wheat and other crops to feed many people. Baghdad became a thriving city. It contained great mosques and palaces for the caliphs. There were large government buildings for the Abbasid government officials and plush homes for wealthy Muslim merchants.

Nevertheless, the Muslim conquests proved to be much too large for one leader to rule. Spain, called al-Andalus, was located thousands of miles away from Baghdad. Al-Andalus soon became independent with its own government. Egypt had also become independent. From its capital, Cairo, Egypt had been ruled by a Muslim dynasty known as the Fatimids since the tenth century. The Fatimids were named after Fatima, the daughter of Muhammad. She had been married to the fourth caliph, Ali ibn Abi Talib, Muhammad's cousin. He ruled from 656 to 661. Some Muslims did not think Ali should be caliph.

There was a civil war in which Ali was defeated by a family called the Umayyad. Members of this family became the new caliphs. Most Muslims recognized their rule and became known as Sunni Muslims. Those who felt Ali and his descendants were the legitimate caliphs became known as Shi'ites.

SELJUK TURKS AND THE CRUSADES

Muslim caliphs supported a flourishing culture in the Islamic world. Cities like Baghdad and Aleppo, located in present-day Syria, were wealthy trading centers. They linked Asia with the Mediterranean Sea. Muslim farmers in the Tigris-Euphrates areas and along the Nile River produced large wheat crops. The wheat was turned into bread to feed hundreds of thousands of people. Farmers also grew a wide variety of fruit, sugarcane, rice, and cotton. The caliphs taxed the farmers and the merchants to pay for their expensive courts and their large armies. Some of these merchants were Jews. They were permitted to practice their religion. But they had to pay an extra tax to the Muslim government in return for not being required to serve in the army. Christians, too, were welcomed but also taxed more heavily than Muslims.

With their large incomes, Muslim caliphs built mosques and religious shrines. They also supported the arts. During the tenth century, the Arabic writer Al-Mutanabbi produced brilliant poetry in praise of Muslim rulers in Baghdad and Cairo. Muslim historians, like al-Tabari and al-Masudi, wrote histories of the Persians, the Egyptians, and the Turks.

During the eleventh century, a tribe of Sunni Muslim warriors, known as the Seljuk Turks, conquered Iran. They marched westward, conquering Baghdad in 1055. However, the Seljuk leaders did not replace the Abbasid caliph. Instead, he remained as head of the government, making a smoother transition for the new rulers. According to historian Albert Hourani, the Turkish leaders did not regard themselves as caliphs, successors to Muhammad. Instead they called themselves sultans, "holders of power."[2]

The Seljuk sultans did not stop with the conquest of Baghdad. They moved northward to challenge the Byzantine Empire. This was a powerful Christian state that had been established over five hundred years earlier. From their capital at Constantinople on the Black Sea, Byzantine emperors ruled a large area. It stretched into Anatolia (present-day Turkey) and westward into Greece. In 1071, however, the Byzantine armies were defeated at the Battle of Manzikert by the Seljuk Turks. Byzantine forces were led into a trap. They were cut to pieces by Muslim cavalry. As a result, Anatolia fell to the Turks, and Constantinople seemed threatened.

Byzantine Emperor Alexius I Comnenus feared that his armies were too weak to defend the kingdom against the Seljuk Turks. Looking westward, Emperor Alexius realized that other Christians might share his fears regarding the Muslims. In Europe, Christians recognized the Pope in Rome as head of their church, called the Catholic Church.

Christians in the Byzantine Empire did not share all the same beliefs as Catholics. Nor did they recognize the Pope as head of Christianity. However, Emperor Alexius and Pope Urban II hoped that Christians might put aside their differences to stop the Muslims.

Late in 1094, Emperor Alexius asked for help from western Europe. It was the Catholic Church that responded. In response to his appeal, Pope Urban issued a call to religious and political leaders of Europe. The pope traveled to Clermont, in central France, to address a large gathering of church leaders. Late in 1095, they met beyond the city in a large field, big enough for the entire crowd. News of the Pope's speech had also been sent across Europe. At Clermont, according to one witness, Pope Urban said:

> I exhort you with earnest prayers, not I, but God, that as heralds of Christ you urge men of all ranks, rich as well as poor, knights as well as foot soldiers, to hasten to exterminate this vile race [Muslims] from the lands of your eastern brethren. . . . Enter upon the road to the Holy Sepulcher, wrest that land from the wicked race and make it subject to yourselves.[3]

Pope Urban then added the words that became the motto of the First Crusade, "God wills it."

Pope Urban called on Christian leaders to undertake this crusade to the Middle East. The First Crusade was designed to drive out the Muslims. Its goal was to retake Jerusalem and safeguard the area for Christianity. Urban hoped that the nobles of Europe would respond to his call.

He promised to forgive their sins if they joined the Crusade. Europe in the eleventh century was divided into small kingdoms and principalities. Each ruler had a small army of mounted cavalry, knights, as well as armed infantry. Many of these rulers saw the Crusade as an opportunity to serve God. They also hoped to acquire some land in the Middle East by defeating the Muslims.

Most of the Crusaders came from France. The Muslims would call them Franks. They were led by Baldwin of Boulogne; Robert II, Count of Flanders; and Raymond IV, Count of Toulouse. The Crusaders traveled with their soldiers to Constantinople in 1096. Meanwhile, the Muslims were divided by conflicts among their leaders. As a result, they were not strong enough to defend their cities. Over the next three years, the Crusaders captured major Muslim cities, including Antioch. Muslim cities along the Mediterranean coast also fell to Crusaders as they approached Jerusalem.

In June 1099, the siege of Jerusalem began. Approximately thirteen thousand Crusaders encircled the city. The Crusaders moved up giant catapults, called *magonels*. The magonels hurled rocks at the city walls to batter them down. The Crusaders also built giant siege towers. These were moved by heavy wooden wheels toward Jerusalem. Knights positioned themselves on top of the towers and shot arrows at the defenders on the walls of the city. The Muslims defending Jerusalem relied on their own magonels as well as a weapon known as Greek fire. Greek fire was a sort of crude oil, known as *naphtha*. The oil was placed in pots, set on fire, and hurled from a

Today, Jerusalem is a mixture of ancient and modern buildings.

magonel. The Greek fire also contained sulfur, which made it stick to anything it struck. When the Greek fire hit enemy catapults or siege towers, the wooden machines were set ablaze.

The siege of Jerusalem continued for more than a month. Eventually, the Christians wheeled their siege towers up to the walls of Jerusalem. On top of the towers were Christian knights. The knights lowered wooden bridges from the towers onto the city walls. Then the knights clambered over them, cutting down the Muslim defenders. A bloodbath followed inside Jerusalem. Christian soldiers killed innocent Muslim women and children, while also slaughtering Jews. Bishop Daimbert of Pisa, Italy, who accompanied the Crusaders, later wrote the Pope, "If you desire to know what was done with the enemy who were found there, know that . . . our men rode in the blood of Saracens [Muslims] up to the knees of their horses."[4]

MUSLIMS AND CHRISTIANS

Following the victory at Jerusalem in 1099, the Crusaders established a series of small states. They were called Outremer, meaning the "land across the seas." Outremer included Antioch along the Mediterranean Sea in the north. On its eastern border lay the County of Edessa. Southward along the Mediterranean was the County of Tripoli, conquered in 1109. The Kingdom of Jerusalem itself stretched from Beirut (the capital of present-day Lebanon) in the north, southward to the town of Eilat on the Gulf of Aqaba.

The Crusader states created a serious threat to the Muslim leaders. But local rulers, called *emirs*, were protective of their own authority. They did not want to take orders from Damascus and join a united assault on Jerusalem or other Christian strongholds. These rulers refused to support each other. Instead they tried to make peace with the Christians. It was not until the 1130s that a strong Muslim military commander appeared to lead a *jihad*, Muslim holy war, against the Christians.

This commander was Imad al-Din Zengi. He was governor of Mosul, located in present-day Iraq. Beginning in 1135, Zengi captured several castles defended by the Christian knights. Four years later, Zengi captured Baalbek, controlled by a Muslim prince allied to the Christians. After the city fell, Zengi had appointed Ayyub, the father of Saladin, governor of the city. In 1144, Zengi gathered enough soldiers to attack the Christian stronghold of Edessa. Zengi's soldiers surrounded the city, and huge catapults hurled boulders against Edessa's walls. Meanwhile, Muslim soldiers dug tunnels under the walls, which were designed to weaken the walls. When the defenders of Edessa refused to surrender, the wooden beams supporting the roofs of the tunnels were set on fire. Part of Edessa's walls collapsed. Zengi's soldiers then rushed into the city. Because the people of Edessa had broken an earlier promise to support Zengi and instead rebelled against him, he allowed his men to massacre the defenders.

MOSUL

Mosul was an important city in the Middle East during Saladin's reign. In the ancient world it was known as Nimrud. For several centuries, Mosul was part of the Roman Empire. In the seventh century A.D., it was conquered by the Muslims. Mosul became a vital trading center, linking the Mediterranean world with Persia and India. After Saladin's death, Mosul was destroyed by the invading Mongols in the thirteenth century. Two centuries later, it was conquered by the Ottoman Turks. They controlled the city until the end of World War I. During the twentieth century, Mosul became part of the modern nation of Iraq.

Two years later, Zengi was assassinated. He was succeeded by his son, Nur al-Din. According to historian Aamin Maalouf, Nur al-Din employed a group of religious leaders to win support for himself in Syria. They preached about his religious principles. These included "a single religion, Sunni Islam, which meant a determined struggle against all the various 'heresies'; a single state that would encircle the [Crusaders] on all fronts; a single objective, [jihad], to reconquer the occupied territories and above all to liberate Jerusalem."[5] Among the Muslims, Nur al-Din was revered as a highly religious leader.

In 1146, Christian knights had launched the Second Crusade from Europe. Led by King Conrad III of Germany and Louis VII of France, the Crusaders set out for Damascus. The Crusader army approached the city in

July 1149. Damascus was defended by a series of walls that surrounded dense orchards. The Crusaders, however, succeeded in defeating the Muslim defenders along the outer walls. Then the Crusaders headed toward the main defenses closer to the city. The attack was difficult because of the dense orchards along part of the city walls. So the Crusaders decided to strike at another section of the city's defenses. As the Crusaders changed position, they received word that Nur al-Din was approaching with a huge army. As Muslim historian, Ibn al-Qalanisi, who wrote during the twelfth century, explained, "News reached the [Christians] . . . that the Muslims were bearing down on them to attack them and wipe them out, and they felt defeat was certain. They consulted among themselves and

DAMASCUS

Damascus was one of the largest cities in the Muslim empire. According to historian P. H. Newby, the city included:

> a large free hospital, twenty colleges for students of law and religion. . . . The Orthodox Christian church, St. Mary's was brilliant with mosaics, and worshippers there were freely allowed to follow their religion. The rich Jewish community of some 3,000, many of them refugees from the Latin Kingdom of Jerusalem, ran their own university.[6]

The center of life in Damascus was the Great Mosque, filled with beautiful mosaics showing images of paradise. From the three *minarets*, or towers on the mosque, Muslims were called to prayers five times daily.

As a youth, Saladin (right) enjoyed playing polo. This was one way that he learned the skills needed to fight from a horse.

decided that the only way to escape from the abyss that loomed ahead . . . was to take flight. At dawn the following day they retreated in miserable confusion and disorder."[7]

The Second Crusade had ended with a great triumph for Nur al-Din. Meanwhile, Saladin's family continued to serve the caliph. Nur al-Din appointed Saladin's father, Ayyub, governor of Damascus. At fourteen, in 1152, Saladin went to Aleppo where he received military training under his uncle. By 1156, Saladin had been transferred to Damascus where he served in the Muslim government. Shortly afterward, he became an important aid to Nur al-Din. According to historian Andrew Ehrenkreutz, Saladin and Nur al-Din were excellent horsemen who enjoyed playing polo together.[8] This game is played by men on horseback. They use long-handled mallets to drive a ball into their opponent's goal.

In 1162, Nur al-Din asked Saladin to join his uncle on an important campaign against the Fatimids in Egypt. This campaign changed Saladin's career.

Saladin in Egypt and Syria

SALADIN GAINED VALUABLE EXPERIENCE AS A political and military leader in Egypt. Then he advanced northward and took over the government in Syria.

During the twelfth century, the Fatimid caliphs faced a serious crisis. Egypt was continually threatened by the Crusader states. Their ships attacked Egyptian ports, like Alexandria, the ancient capital of Egypt. The Crusaders also built fortresses that threatened trade routes between Egypt and Syria. Fatimid rulers were unable to assemble an army powerful enough to defeat the Crusaders. In 1160, Caliph al-Faiz died, leaving the throne to his eleven-year-old son, al-Adid. He lacked the experience to run the country. Instead, al-Adid left the administration in the hands of his chief minister, known as a *wazir*. This position was so important that several men contended for it. No sooner did one become wazir than he was assassinated or driven out by his opponent.

In 1163, a wazir named Shawar was driven out by another government official named Dirgham. Shawar fled to Syria and asked Nur al-Din to put him back in power. Nur al-Din realized that he might use this situation to his own advantage. He might be able to bring an army into Egypt and take control of the country. Then he could mount an attack on the Christian kingdoms from two different directions—Syria and Egypt. In 1164, Nur al-Din ordered Shirkuh to lead an expedition into Egypt. Shirkuh was accompanied by his nephew Saladin.

EXPEDITIONS TO EGYPT

Shirkuh's invasion was highly successful. Dirgham's army was no match for the highly trained Syrians. They defeated the Egyptians at Bilbais, north of Cairo, in May 1164. Dirgham was killed, and Shawar was reinstalled as wazir. Following the victory, Shawar was expected to pay Shirkuh and his soldiers for returning him to power. But Shawar refused to carry out his part of the bargain. In July, Shirkuh defeated Shawar and the troops he had been able to gather together. To save his position, Shawar decided to contact the Crusaders in the kingdom of Jerusalem. He concluded a deal with them to invade Egypt and drive out Shirkuh. Led by Almaric, the king of Jerusalem, they marched into Egypt and besieged the city of Bilbais. But because Bilbais had been heavily supplied by Saladin, it held out against the Crusaders. The armies commanded by

Almaric and Shirkuh were so evenly matched that neither could win a victory. Therefore, both of them finally decided to leave Egyptian territory.

Shirkuh returned to Damascus. But he did not forget what had happened in Egypt. In 1167, he persuaded Nur al-Din to send him back so he could take his revenge on Shawar. With Saladin as his second-in-command, Shirkuh invaded Egypt. Once inside the country, he faced an army of Christians and Egyptians. They were commanded by Almaric and Shawar. At the Battle of al-Babain, fought in April 1167, Shirkuh won a decisive victory against the enemy. Saladin played a key role in the battle. Shirkuh had placed him in charge of defending the Syrian supply camp. He hoped that the enemy might attack Saladin and be lured into a trap. Once the attack was under way, Shirkuh planned to fall on the Egyptian-Christian army in the rear and defeat them. The enemy fell into Shirkuh's trap. Saladin's stout defense of the supply camp gave time to Shirkuh to attack, making victory possible.

The Syrians then occupied Alexandria. Saladin was placed in charge of defending the ancient city. Meanwhile, Shirkuh headed south to recruit reinforcements for his army. His forces had been reduced by the battle at al-Babain. While Saladin was at Alexandria, he was besieged by Almaric and Shawar. Saladin successfully held out against the attack. During the siege, Shirkuh returned with his army to threaten the enemy. But, after al-Babain, the Christians and Muslims did not want to fight another bloody battle. Therefore, Almaric retreated from Egypt.

In return, Saladin and his troops were permitted to leave Alexandria in safety.

As a result of his successful performance in Egypt, Saladin's reputation grew in Syria. When he returned, the young commander was hailed as a hero of the campaign. However, the Syrians had still failed to secure control of Egypt. In 1168, the Crusaders invaded Egypt again, hoping to take control of the country for themselves. This time Caliph al-Adid asked for help from Nur al-Din. Saladin was not eager to return to Egypt. As he put it, "What I went through in Alexandria I shall never forget."[1] Nevertheless, Saladin finally agreed to go to Egypt at the request of Nur al-Din.

This time Shirkuh commanded a combined force of Syrians and Egyptians that was too powerful for the Crusaders. In 1169, Almaric retreated from Egypt. But Shirkuh made sure that the wazir Shawar would never join with the Christians again. Nor would he bring them back as he did in 1164 and 1167. Shawar was captured by Saladin and executed.

SALADIN, THE NEW WAZIR

In Shawar's place, the caliph named Shirkuh to become the new wazir in Egypt. Shortly after taking on this position, however, Shirkuh over ate at a lavish banquet and suddenly died. He was succeeded by his nephew, Saladin, who was selected by Nur al-Din. In 1169, at thirty, Saladin became wazir and commander of the Syrian and Egyptian armies. Suddenly, Saladin found himself dressed in the lavish white and gold turban of a wazir. He also carried a magnificent sword as a symbol of his office. Historian Karen Armstrong wrote:

> A sensitive man, Saladin found this astonishing and even shocking: he, who had not wanted to come to Egypt at all, was now its honored vizier. He could only explain it as the will of God: he must have a divine calling. From the moment he was [selected] wazir, Saladin was a transformed man. He had a religious conversion and started to live a very devout [religious] life.[2]

Saladin began to study with Muslim clerics. Baha al-Din, the biographer and companion of Saladin, said that both of them prayed together regularly. Baha al-Din spent many years serving Saladin and observed him closely. He said that Saladin "loved to hear the noble Koran recited . . . and used often to be moved to tears by hearing the Koran. . . ."[3]

In his new position as wazir, Saladin supported the policies of the young Fatimid caliph. As an outsider, Saladin did not have wide support among Egyptians. To strengthen his position inside Egypt, he needed to work with the Fatimid leaders, not against them. Nevertheless, Nur al-Din did not always agree with Saladin's approach to his new job. As historian P. H. Newby wrote, Nur al-Din wanted to have Egypt and Syria united in a holy war against the Crusaders. He also expected that the Egyptian government would send Syria large sums of money. This could be used to help build the Muslim armies for an invasion of the Crusader states. Saladin saw things differently.

He believed that as wazir, his first responsibility was to build the strength of Egypt. Then the Egyptians could withstand another Crusader invasion.[4]

Saladin's first threat, however, came not from the Crusaders but from inside Egypt. Soldiers loyal to the Fatimid caliph revolted at Cairo in 1169. Saladin harshly put down the revolt. In fact, he ordered his soldiers to burn down the houses where families of the Egyptian troops were living. As the Egyptians saw their families being killed, they retreated. But the battle continued house to house. Historian Andrew Ehrenkreutz wrote, "To destroy nests of resistance, the pursuing troops had to burn house after house sheltering the fleeing [enemy]."[5]

About the same time, Saladin had to deal with another invasion by the Crusaders. Their ships approached the Egyptian port of Damietta on the Nile Delta. Saladin's soldiers succeeded in driving back the attack, and the Crusaders left Egypt. Meanwhile, Saladin had received reinforcements in Egypt from Nur al-Din. Al-Din finally recognized how critical the situation was there. These reinforcements arrived under the leadership of Saladin's brothers, Turanshah, Tughtigin, and Shams al-Dawlah. Saladin immediately put his three brothers into important positions in the Egyptian army. In 1170, he was also joined by his father Ayyub. Saladin had so much respect for his father that he offered him the position of wazir. But Ayyub refused. "God would not have chosen you for this great position if you had not been fitted for it," he said.[6]

That same year, Saladin began a campaign against the Crusaders. His goal was to capture the Crusader stronghold at Eilat on the Gulf of Aqaba. This was the southern border of the kingdom of Jerusalem. To prevent Almaric from concentrating reinforcements there to defeat him, Saladin planned a diversionary movement. He led his troops to Darum, a Crusader stronghold that was located north of Egypt. Almaric sent a relief force to drive off Saladin. The wazir slipped away at night and struck the Crusader town of Gaza. As Almaric was trying to deal with this attack, Saladin's armies struck Eilat and captured it in December 1170.

Nine months later, in September 1171, Egypt faced another crisis. The caliph al-Adid died. His son, a boy of about ten, expected to become the new caliph. But Saladin had no intention of letting him take power. "I am the deputy of your father in the matters of the caliphate," Saladin reportedly said. "And he did not order me to make you his successor." Instead, Saladin himself became head of the government. At the same time, he proclaimed an end to the Shi'ite form of Islamic worship in Egypt and replaced it with Sunnism.

SALADIN IN CHARGE OF EGYPT

In Egypt, Saladin continued to pursue a course that was relatively independent from Nur al-Din. Saladin sent some money from the Egyptian treasury to Damascus. But it was never enough to satisfy Nur al-Din. Meanwhile, Saladin sold off many of the expensive jewels and other items owned by the Fatimids to pay for a larger army. Saladin was interested in the defense of Egypt. He believed that Almaric was allying the Christians with the Byzantine Empire and together they would attack Egypt. Nur al-Din, on the other hand, saw Egypt as a part of his grand strategy of driving out the Christians. He wanted to squeeze them between the Egyptian and Syrian armies.

In pursuit of his own policy, Saladin began to expand the Egyptian border. In 1173, he invaded the Crusader lands located around the fortress of Kerak near the Dead Sea. But this expedition was cut short by a tragedy in Egypt. According to historian Andrew Ehrenkreutz, Saladin's father fell off his horse on July 31, 1173. Najm al-Din Ayyub died just over a week later, before Saladin could return to his bedside. It was a great loss for Saladin.[7]

Soon afterward, Saladin returned to his policies of expansion. In 1174, he sent his armies in an attack on Yemen along the Red Sea. His soldiers, led by Shams al-Dawlah, captured the wealthy port city of Aden. This city traded with India, Africa, and the Middle East. The trade could greatly increase the wealth of Egypt. At home, Saladin was forced to put down a revolt among political leaders who supported the Fatimids. This revolt had barely ended when Saladin received the news that Nur al-Din had died in Damascus.

Saladin had often acted independently of Nur al-Din. This brought the two men into conflict. In part, they disagreed over the policy in Egypt. Historian Karen Armstrong believed that another issue divided the two men. Saladin "believed that God had called *him*, not Nur al-Din, to liberate Palestine and this seems to have caused Saladin a great deal of perplexity. If he fought under Nur

Saladin's Fortress on the Mountain still stands today. Over the centuries, builders have added to it; however, the original walls built in Saladin's time are pictured above.

al-Din's banner this would be to surrender what he firmly believed to be his divine mission. . . ."[8]

LEADER OF SYRIA

The death of Nur al-Din created uncertainty in the Muslim world. He was succeeded by his son, a child named al-Salih. Powerful leaders in Syria maneuvered to take over the government. In Damascus, some of these men tried to control al-Salih and rule in his name. A rival group in Mosul refused to recognize the authority of Damascus. Mosul was ruled by Sayf al-Din Ghazi, Nur al-Din's nephew. Another powerful group, in charge of the fortress city of Aleppo, also wanted to control al-Salih. Eventually al-Salih and his advisors decided to move from Damascus to Aleppo. However, many of the military leaders in Damascus were unhappy with this move. Therefore, they called on Saladin to march northward from Egypt to take control of the situation in Syria.

Saladin headed north with seven hundred of his cavalry. He arrived in Damascus in October 1174. There he was hailed as the new ruler of the city. According to historian Karen Armstrong,

> Saladin's greatest strength was that his new religious fervor enabled him to present himself to the common people as a devout Muslim ruler . . . He was not only scrupulous about living frugally and giving alms [money to the poor] generously, but he was a shining example of the accessibility that a Muslim ruler should have vis-à-vis the people. . . . He always ate with his soldiers. . . . He never

DAMASCUS UNDER SALADIN

Damascus, the center of Saladin's empire, is a very old city. It was part of the Egyptian Empire in the ancient world. During the fourth century B.C., the city was captured by the armies of Alexander the Great. In 64 B.C., Damascus was conquered by Roman armies, led by Pompey the Great. For several centuries, Damascus remained part of the Roman Empire. The city was conquered by Muslim armies in the seventh century, becoming the capital of the new Islamic Empire. Muslim rulers built beautiful mosques and palaces in the city. The Seljuk Turks conquered Damascus in the eleventh century.

Under the leadership of Nur al-Din, the Muslims successfully defended the city from a Crusader attack. Nur al-Din improved the city. He built a religious school in Damascus, a public bath and a hospital. In addition, he began the building of the Shams al-Muluk palace. Saladin continued the work of Nur al-Din at Damascus.

After Saladin's death, the city was ruled by his son, al-Afdal. In 1260, Damascus fell to an invasion by the Mongols. But they were quickly driven out by the Mamluks. Damascus became part of their empire that was ruled from Egypt. They built many mosques in Damascus as well as minarets. In the sixteenth century, Damascus was conquered by the Ottoman Turks. They held the city until their defeat in World War I. In the twentieth century, Damascus became the capital of the modern nation of Syria. Saladin is buried in Damascus at the Omayyad Mosque. Two large pillars stand near his mausoleum. One of the pillars is made of wood and the other is constructed from marble.

demanded special treatment. . . . But it was his devotion to the holy war . . . against the [Christian Crusaders] that did more than anything else to convince the people that Saladin was a worthy successor to the great Nur al-Din.[9]

But before this war could begin, Saladin had to deal with other issues. He realized that peace in Syria was impossible while Aleppo continued under the control of al-Salih and his advisors. In December, Saladin led his army against Aleppo. He began to lay siege to the city. Severe winter weather made the operation extremely difficult. During the campaign, Saladin was almost assassinated. The assassins were hired by al-Salih and his advisors in Aleppo. Fortunately, the assassination was discovered at the last minute. One of Saladin's emirs was killed trying to defend him. Another Muslim soldier stepped in and beheaded the assassin.

Saladin was unable to take control of Aleppo. He retreated from the city in January 1175. Meanwhile, he called up reinforcements from Egypt to strengthen his position in Syria. In April, an army from Aleppo advanced against Saladin, hoping to defeat him. Both armies met at the Horns of Hamah in April 1175. The Egyptian reinforcements arrived just in time to swing the battle in Saladin's favor, giving him a decisive victory. Leaders at Aleppo agreed to join forces with Saladin to fight against the Crusaders. They no longer supported al-Salih as the caliph of Damascus.

This agreement was only a short pause in the civil war between Saladin and his opponents. Soon afterward, the

ASSASSINS

During the twelfth century, paid assassins operated out of a mountain top fortress in Quadmus, located in present-day Syria. Actually called the Assassins, they were a small group of Shi'ites who opposed the Sunni form of Islam. They were dedicated to defeating the Seljuk rulers.

The Assassins were started by Hasan as-Sabah in the eleventh century. During the twelfth century they were led by Sinan, who was called the Old Man of the Mountain. In Arabic, the word for assassin is *hashishyun*. This is the origin of the word hashish, the name of a drug that was smoked by the Assassins. Under the influence of hashish, the young Assassins were more eager to undertake the murder of a political leader like Saladin. The Shi'ite Assassins were convinced that if they died, they would be rewarded for trying to kill a Sunni. The reward would be spending eternity in paradise.

Saladin escaped several assassination attempts. But other leaders were not so lucky. The Assassins killed a wazir and two caliphs. By the mid-twelfth century, there were an estimated forty thousand Assassins. They controlled a large area that bordered the principality of Antioch.

leaders of Aleppo began planning another attempt to stop Saladin. They hoped to ally themselves with Mosul and drive Saladin out of Syria. Saladin learned of this new plan. He called in more troops from Egypt to stop it. In April 1176, Saladin's army met the combined forces of Mosul and Aleppo at Tel al-Sultan. The soldiers from Mosul and Aleppo were commanded by Sayf al-Din. Early in the battle, Saladin's forces on the left flank were pushed back by the enemy. But Saladin himself spearheaded a crushing cavalry attack. This turned the tide and drove his enemies from the field. Sayf al-Din was lucky to escape with his life. When Saladin's troops entered his camp, they found it "to be more like a tavern, with all its wines, guitars, lute bands and singing girls," according to an account written at the time.[10] In other words, Sayf al-Din's followers were not good Muslims.

Soon afterward, Saladin besieged the important fortress of Azaz in northern Syria. It fell to his armies in June 1176. Saladin was still unable to defeat Aleppo. Nevertheless, most of Syria and all of Egypt were now under his control. He had proclaimed a new government, now known as the Ayyubid Dynasty.

BATTLING THE CRUSADERS IN EGYPT AND PALESTINE

While Saladin was strengthening his empire, he did not lose sight of Christian enemies lurking on his borders. The Byzantine Empire to the north and the Crusader kingdoms to the south still menaced the Muslims. Fortunately for

Saladin, the Byzantines had been weakened by battles against the Muslims in Asia Minor. Meanwhile, Almaric, the king of Jerusalem, had died in 1174. His son, Baldwin, became king. But he was a sickly boy. Baldwin IV suffered from leprosy. This disease is caused by bacteria that create severe sores on a leper's skin. As a result, Baldwin was not strong enough to lead an attack against the Muslims. Therefore, the threats from Byzantium and Jerusalem were greatly reduced.

In 1176, Saladin returned to Egypt. Although there was no immediate threat from the Crusaders, he began building up the Egyptian fleet for the future. In November 1177, Saladin invaded the Crusader kingdoms around the area of Gaza. However, his army was caught off guard by a swift Crusader attack. Many of his soldiers were slaughtered, and Saladin almost lost his life. The following year, a Crusader army attacked the Muslim city of Hamah in

SALADIN'S MARRIAGE

Before leaving for Egypt in 1176, Saladin married Ismat al-Din. She was a widow of Nur al-Din. According to historian P. H. Newby, "From the earliest days of Islam it had been accepted that the conquest of a state was consummated by possession of the former monarch's wife or daughter . . . the marriage provided a certain status, perhaps a degree of legitimacy [for Saladin] in the eyes of Syrians. . . ."[11] Saladin had several wives, which was the custom for Muslim men at the time. He had an estimated seventeen children.

southern Syria. But the Crusaders were beaten back by the defenders of Hamah in a bloody battle.

In 1179, Saladin led another invasion of the Crusader kingdoms. He attacked an area near Beirut. There he won a major victory in the battle against the Crusaders. According to historian Andrew Ehrenkreutz, Saladin captured more than two hundred seventy Christian knights. "Most were later ransomed for huge sums of gold—a much welcomed revenue to finance Saladin's war effort."[12] Meanwhile, the Muslim fleet attacked Crusader strongholds. In October, they entered the harbor outside the city of Acre on the Mediterranean coast. The Muslim invaders destroyed the Christian ships in the harbor before heading back to Egypt.

Saladin returned to Egypt in 1181. He had placed his brother, Shams al-Dawlah, in charge of Alexandria. But Shams al-Dawlah had died in 1180. After his return, Saladin built up the fortifications at several important Egyptian cities, including Alexandria and Damietta. Meanwhile, he sent his brother Sayf al-Din Tughtigin to Yemen as governor.

RETURN TO SYRIA

In Egypt, Saladin was informed that Sultan al-Salih, age nineteen, had died in Aleppo. Before his death in December 1181, al-Salih had named Izz al-Din, leader of Mosul, as his successor. (Izz al-Din had replaced his brother Sayf al-Din, who had died in 1180.) Izz al-Din traveled to Aleppo to bind the city in an alliance with

SALADIN'S SIEGE ENGINES

Saladin's siege engines were based on designs used by the Romans in the ancient world. One of these devices was called the *ballista*. It was designed like a giant cross bow. The ballista shot a huge, heavy arrow against a castle wall.

Another siege engine was called the catapult or magonel. This comes from a Greek word that means engine of war. The magonel had a single arm, hollowed out at one end. Ropes pulled back the arm. The hollowed end was filled with a large boulder. In addition, armies filled the hollowed section with flaming materials or dead animals. When the ropes were released, the boulder, flaming material, or dead animal was hurled toward the enemy castle. The projectile could destroy parts of the castle or kill enemy soldiers on the walls. Dead animals could spread disease among enemy troops.

A third type of siege engine used during the Crusades was the *trebuchet*. This was an invention of the French during the twelfth century, the same period as the Third Crusade. Instead of twisting ropes to create tension, the trebuchet relied on a heavy weight in a box or basket placed at one end. On the other end, the trebuchet contained a sling that could hold a rock up to three hundred pounds in weight. This was a much heavier projectile than the magonel or the ballista could hurl. A large boulder hurled by the trebuchet could knock out a castle tower. The sling gave the trebuchet extra range. A boulder could be fired against a castle from a distance of as far as three hundred yards. When the arm containing the sling was released, it rapidly lifted into the air from the weight of the heavy box or basket on the other end. Trebuchets gradually replaced other types of siege engines because they were much more powerful.

Mosul. Saladin regarded this alliance as a threat to his own rule in Syria. Therefore, he returned to Syria in 1182. Soon afterward, he began a campaign against small cities in Syria that were friendly to Aleppo and Mosul. Many of them, instead of submitting to a bloody siege, threw their support to Saladin.

By the end of the year, Saladin had approached Mosul and begun a siege of the city. But the city's defenses, with their thick walls and high towers, were too strong for Saladin's army. As a result, he finally withdrew from the city and attacked the nearby fortress of Sinjar. It fell to Saladin at the end of December 1182.

His focus on Syria, however, created an opportunity for the Crusaders. In January 1183, Crusader ships appeared in the Red Sea. They attacked the Muslim stronghold of Eilat in Egypt and struck Muslim ships operating in the Red Sea. The Crusader attack also threatened important cities on the Arabian peninsula, such as Mecca. Saladin's army and navy in Egypt were under the leadership of his brother al-Adil. He attacked the Crusader vessels, which were destroyed. Nevertheless, these battles emphasized the fact that the Crusaders presented a constant threat to the Muslim cities.

In 1183, Saladin made another attempt to capture Aleppo. This time his siege was successful and he took control of the city.

Two years later, Saladin began a campaign against Mosul, ruled by Izz al-Din. While he was in the midst of siege, however, Saladin became very sick. He ordered his army to retreat until he could recover. Nevertheless,

ALEPPO

Aleppo, a key stronghold in Saladin's empire, is one of the oldest cities in the world. Aleppo was already a thriving trading center during the third millenium B.C. Trade routes passed through Aleppo from the Mediterranean Sea to the Tigris and Euphrates rivers. During the second millenium, the city was controlled by the Hittites and the Egyptians. Later, it was part of the Persian Empire until it was conquered by the Romans in the first century B.C.

The Muslims conquered Aleppo in the seventh century A.D. A large castle was built on a hill in the center of Aleppo to defend the city from attack. As a result, the Crusaders were unable to capture the city. Under the Muslims, Aleppo became a cultural center, known for its art and poetry. During the twelfth century, much of Aleppo was destroyed by an earthquake that struck the city. Nur al Din rebuilt large sections of Aleppo, including the castle that defended it from the Crusaders. The Muslim leader also established a religious school in Aleppo and he built a large mosque in the city.

Saladin regarded Aleppo as an important city and placed his brother in charge of it. After Saladin's death, his son, al-Zahir made improvements in the city. He added a new entrance bridge and a moat around the citadel. Over the next few centuries, Aleppo was invaded repeatedly. The Mongols burned the city in 1260. For several centuries, Aleppo was part of the Mamluk Empire, governed from Egypt. In the sixteenth century, the Ottomans defeated the Mamluk armies just outside Aleppo. The new rulers constructed additional mosques in the city. They also built inns, called *khans*, as well as magnificent homes with beautiful courtyards. The Ottomans ruled Aleppo until their defeat in the First World War. During the twentieth century, Aleppo became part of the modern nation of Syria.

representatives of Izz al-Din agreed to a peace treaty with Saladin. They recognized him as the Ayyubid sultan of Syria. Most of Syria was now united under Saladin. He was at last ready to concentrate on the Crusader kingdoms. This would lead to a hard-fought war that would determine the dominant power in the area.

THE CRUSADER KINGDOMS

THE CRUSADERS WHO JOURNEYED TO THE HOLY
Land in the eleventh century went for a variety of reasons.
They wanted to serve God by reconquering Jerusalem and
possibly achieve a place for themselves in heaven. They
also hoped to acquire land and perhaps even some
treasures of gold and silver. But after Jerusalem was
conquered, many returned to Europe. They found that
there was not much fertile land or golden treasure. They
had also fulfilled their mission of serving God. Some
Crusaders, however, remained in the Holy Land, and this
experience changed their lives forever.

Shortly after the fall of Jerusalem in 1099, Godfrey of
Bouillon was selected by the other leaders of the Crusade
as the new ruler of the city. Godfrey was a very religious
man who felt uncomfortable being called a king.
Therefore, he used the title Protector of the Holy
Sepulcher. Godfrey died in 1100 and he was succeeded by
his brother, Baldwin. As historian Angus Konstam wrote,

Baldwin "had no reservations about calling himself king of Jerusalem. When he was crowned on Christmas Day, 1100, he became the . . . head of a feudal state, not a mere defender of the Church."[1] Baldwin expanded the kingdom, conquering Muslim cities along the coast. These included Beirut, Tyre, and Acre. Baldwin also tried to assert control over other Crusader states, like Antioch and Tripoli. But they remained independent.

THE KINGDOM OF JERUSALEM

The kingdom of Jerusalem, like the other Crusader states, was organized according to a system called feudalism. This was the same system that existed in western Europe. In the kingdom of Jerusalem, as in Europe, the king governed through a group of vassals. He gave each of them some land, called a fief. In turn, his vassals promised to serve in the king's army and help defend the kingdom. Each vassal was a powerful noble. He, in turn, had his own vassals serving in his army and defending his land. When war broke out, each noble gathered his vassals together and marched off to join the king's army.

The government of the Crusader states lay in the hands of the king, the powerful nobles, and the Christian bishops. These men served as advisors to the king. They formed a high court, called a *haute cour*. The high court acted as a check on the king's power. They decided how much money he should receive from tax revenues to run his royal court in Jerusalem. They also called out the army when the kingdom was threatened by invasion. In

This type of gold coin, called a *bezant*, was issued by a Crusader king about a hundred years before Saladin's time.

addition, the haute cour served as a court of law that heard important cases in the kingdom. However, the high court became corrupt. The nobles undermined the power of the king. They refused to give him any taxes or military aid beyond the minimum amount.

Nobles supported themselves by collecting taxes from the peasants who farmed the land. Each peasant presented part of his harvest to a noble lord, who sold it for cash. However, the dry climate of Jerusalem did not produce a large amount of fertile land. Therefore, many noble vassals were given towns and cities by the king. The king kept Jerusalem as his own source of income. But he gave his vassals cities such as Beirut, Sidon, Haifa, Nablus, and Hebron. The vassals collected taxes from merchants and craftsmen who lived in the cities. Each city was a busy trading center, where as many as one hundred ships could be seen in the harbor. Spices from the Far East were shipped to these Mediterranean ports. From there, they went to western Europe. Some merchants sold rich dyes that were sent to Italy. There the dye was used to color clothing of Italian wool. Traders also bought fine quality silks shipped from East Asia, as well as perfumes and fruits grown in the Mediterranean region.

DEFENDING THE CRUSADER KINGDOMS

During the twelfth century, more Europeans came to live in the Crusader kingdoms. They married other Christians who lived in the Holy Land. These new immigrants included Byzantines from Constantinople, Greeks, and

Italian merchants. Approximately two hundred fifty thousand Christians lived in the Crusader states. There were five times that many Muslims living inside these territories. In addition, millions more were living outside the Crusader kingdoms.[2] According to historian Joshua Prawer, the Crusaders made no effort to convert the Muslims to Christianity or to replace them with new immigrants. "Conversion never became a part of the Crusader program, and the waves of European migration never allowed wholesale replacement of the native population by European colonists."[3]

Instead, the Crusaders relied on their own small Christian armies to defend their kingdoms. Prawer estimated that the kingdom of Jerusalem had an army of about six hundred knights and six thousand infantry. While these armies seem small, "in the Middle Ages," according to Prawer, "the heavily mailed, mounted knight had approximately the same combat effectiveness as a modern tank."[4]

Knights did not wear heavy armor, which was introduced much later in the Middle Ages. Instead, they wore coats of chain mail. These were thin strips of metal, formed into rings and linked together into a coat. This coat was called a hauberk. Each knight wore a heavier piece of metal over his head. This was called a helm. Weighing up to twenty-five pounds, it was often shaped like a cylinder, with narrow openings for the knight's eyes. A knight's weapons included a long sword, sharpened on both sides. In addition, knights were skilled at using a bow and arrow to fire at an enemy.

During battles, knights were mounted on powerful warhorses and placed in reserve behind the infantry. The infantry often wore quilted coats. These were not as effective as chain mail in protecting them against the arrows and swords of the enemy. The infantry were armed with spears as well as crossbows, which they relied on for defense. The crossbow fired arrows with greater power than a bowstring. However, the crossbowman could fire about one bolt per six fired by a normal archer. A crossbow's range was also shorter.[5]

In battle, the infantry tried to hold back the enemy, creating a standoff on the battlefield. At this moment, the mounted knights launched a powerful charge. This was designed to break the enemy's ranks and send them fleeing from the battlefield. These knights were considered strong enough to "make a hole through the walls of Babylon," according to a popular saying of the twelfth century.[6]

When knights were not fighting on the battlefield, they were often defending the cities and towns of the Crusader kingdoms. These were ringed by stout walls, designed to withstand a lengthy siege. In addition, the Crusaders constructed castles at strategic points along important roads and trade routes. During the twelfth century, the Crusaders constructed sixty-four castles in the kingdom of Jerusalem.[7] Similar structures were used for defense in Western Europe. In the kingdom of Jerusalem, the line of castles stretched southward from Beirut to the Gulf of Aqaba. The castles were positioned close enough so a signal fire lit at one castle could be seen by another one. These fires were used to warn each castle of an

This Crusader castle in present-day Syria was once raided by Saladin's forces.

approaching enemy. In addition, the Crusaders relied on carrier pigeons to send longer messages. These pigeons were trained to carry a message from one castle to another.

Each castle was designed to hold out during a long siege. Outside the walls, the Crusaders dug a deep ditch. Sometimes it was filled with water to form a moat. This was designed to prevent large siege towers from being wheeled up to the castle walls. Attackers had to fill in the ditches with boulders if they wanted to bring up the towers. Meanwhile, they were pelted with rocks and arrows from defenders on the castle battlements above the ground.

These battlements generally included a series of defensive walls. The outer walls provided the first line of defense. If these walls were overrun by the attackers, the defenders could retreat to a second line of stoutly built walls. These usually included giant towers, too high for ladders to scale. Knights could fire arrows from these towers at the enemy trying to mount the castle walls. The walls themselves were wide flat battlements, large enough for catapults. These could hurl boulders, pots of burning oil, or Greek fire at the enemy. If the second line of defense was breached, the Crusaders had a third line of fortifications. Here they could make a last stand, hoping that reinforcements might arrive to drive off the enemy.

RELIGIOUS ORDERS OF KNIGHTS

Since the number of Crusaders was small, they relied on other soldiers to defend their castles. Many Christian knights made a pledge to fight in the army of Jerusalem for a period of one or two years. They considered this service a religious duty. The Crusaders believed that, in return, their sins would be forgiven by God. The two primary orders of Christian knights were the Knights Hospitallers and the Knights Templars.

The religious Order of Hospitallers was founded during the eleventh century. The order took its name from a hospital started in Jerusalem. The hospital provided care for Christian pilgrims visiting the Holy Land. After Jerusalem was conquered by the Crusaders, the Hospitallers were given lands in the new kingdom. Under the leadership of Raymond of Provence, the Hospitallers grew. "Under the guidance of Father Raymond," according to historian Alan Baker, "the Hospitalers [sic] took vows of poverty, chastity, and obedience, and wore a black mantle [coat] with a white cross on the chest."[8] The kings of Jerusalem also gave the Hospitallers twenty-nine castles that they were expected to defend.

Another military order was the Knights Templars. They were founded in the early twelfth century by Hugh of Payns. He was a knight who had traveled to the Holy Land. Hugh and eight other knights started the order in 1119. They were called the Templars because their headquarters was in Jerusalem, near the Temple of Solomon (a king of Jerusalem in Biblical times). The Templars were warrior monks. They took vows of poverty and pledged to defend the Christian kingdoms against the Muslims. In 1128, Hugh went to western Europe where he appeared at a council of church leaders. There he received the approval of the Catholic Church to expand the

WILLIAM OF TYRE AND THE HISTORY OF THE CRUSADES

Born in Palestine during the 12th century, William became Archbishop of Tyre. This city is located along the Mediterranean coast. William wrote a history of the early crusades, called "Deeds Done Beyond the Sea." Contained in twenty-three books, the history was started around 1170. William's work discussed the Crusades from its beginnings until 1184. Six years later, William died. In one part of the history, William described the early days of the Knights Templars:

> For nine years after their founding, the knights wore secular [regular] clothing. They used such garments as the people, for their soul's salvation, gave them. In their ninth year there was held in France, at Troyes, a council . . . [which] established a rule [set of governing principles] for the knights and assigned them a white habit. Although the knights now had been established for nine years, there were still only nine of them. From this time onward their numbers began to grow and their possessions began to multiply. . . . their wealth is equal to the treasures of kings.[9]

Templars. The order gradually increased as more men joined it. The Templars received lands in Europe as well as in the Crusader kingdoms where they built castles. There may have been as many as four hundred Templar knights during the late twelfth century. Each of them was easy to recognize. He wore a white mantle, or cloak, with a red cross that was part of the Templar uniform.

LIFE IN THE CRUSADER STATES

Most Crusaders, even those with country estates, lived in the cities. They preferred city life in the company of other Europeans rather than being isolated in the countryside. In Europe, homes were generally built of wood. It grew abundantly in forests across the countryside. In the Mediterranean area, there were few forests. Muslims built their houses of stone, surrounded by high walls. These provided privacy for the people who lived in them. The Crusaders lived in the same style of house. In some cases, they took over homes that had belonged to Muslims who had fled following the Christian invasion.

These homes were built of thick stone walls to keep out the heat during summer and preserve warmth during the cold winter months. Each room opened up on a quiet courtyard. It might contain trees and other plantings as well as a fountain. Inside, the rooms were decorated with carpets or tapestries that hung on the walls. The walls might also contain elaborate mosaics—designs made out of small colored stones. These houses were far more elaborately decorated than most houses in Europe during the same period. In addition, most of the Crusaders and their families dressed more lavishly. They wore silks and other expensive fabrics. These were only available to the very rich in Western Europe. Crusaders also adopted the Muslim custom of taking regular baths. Public baths had been built in cities along the Mediterranean. In northern Europe, by contrast, bathing was very rare.

Most Muslims left the cities after the conquest. Those who remained in Outremer lived in the countryside. There, life for most Muslims went on much as before the Crusader invasion. Ibn Jubair, traveling in Palestine during the twelfth century, wrote:

> a road which went through contiguous farms, all inhabited by [Muslims] who live in great prosperity under the Franks [Crusaders from France]. . . . Their obligations are the payment of half the crop at the time of harvest and the payment of a poll-tax [for being Muslims instead of Christian]. . . . The Christians do not demand anything more, but for a light tax on fruit. But the [Muslims] are masters of their habitations and rule themselves as they see fit.[10]

Generally, each town was governed by a Muslim group of elders. They dealt directly with the Christian Crusader who had been given the area as a fief.

KINGS OF JERUSALEM

Each Crusader not only ruled his own fief but was also pledged to support the king. During most of the twelfth century, the kingdom of Jerusalem was ruled by a succession

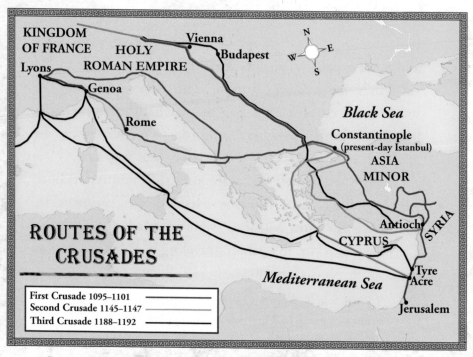

KINGDOM
OF FRANCE   HOLY
            ROMAN EMPIRE
Lyons
    Genoa
        Rome

Vienna
    Budapest

Black Sea
Constantinople
(present-day Istanbul)
ASIA
MINOR

Antioch
CYPRUS

SYRIA

Mediterranean Sea

Tyre
Acre

Jerusalem

ROUTES OF THE CRUSADES

First Crusade 1095–1101
Second Crusade 1145–1147
Third Crusade 1188–1192

Over a period of about one hundred years, European Christians fought Muslims in three major Crusades.

of monarchs related to Baldwin I. Each ruler attempted to control the other kingdoms, like Tripoli and Antioch. However, they remained independent. Almaric, who ruled from 1163 to 1174, tried to expand the Crusader kingdoms into Egypt. He was stopped by Saladin who eventually united Egypt with Syria. Almaric was succeeded by Baldwin IV, a young man who suffered from leprosy. The disease so weakened Baldwin that he died in 1185. Before his death, he asked Raymond of Tripoli, a leading Crusader knight, to become regent. He was expected to run the kingdom for Baldwin's young son, Baldwin V.

However, Baldwin V died a year later, at the age of nine. Many knights wanted Raymond to continue to rule as regent until a new king could be selected. But Baldwin's mother, Sybilla, claimed the kingdom for herself. She proclaimed herself queen and crowned her husband, Guy of Lusignan, as king of Jerusalem. "I make choice of thee as king," she said, "and as my lord, and as lord of the land of Jerusalem, for those whom God hath joined together, let not man put asunder."[11]

Raymond had tried to maintain peace with Saladin and the Muslims. Indeed, Raymond and Saladin had signed a four-year truce in 1184. According to the Koran, a Muslim leader should seek peace, instead of war, if peace is in the interests of Islam. Saladin, therefore, agreed to a peace treaty. But King Guy had arrived in Jerusalem during the 1170s. He wanted to own a large fief for himself. Very little land was available. Therefore, Guy decided to acquire more Muslim lands and thought this could only be accomplished by warfare. Guy was also pressured to go to war by nobles who had recently arrived in Palestine. Many others, especially those on the haute cour, opposed his rule.

Nevertheless, Guy and Sybilla were rulers of the kingdom. With their supporters, they began to pursue a risky foreign policy. It ultimately led to disaster at the hands of Saladin.

SALADIN'S DECISIVE VICTORY

IN THE WINTER OF 1187, A CARAVAN OF MUSLIM travelers left Cairo for Damascus. They rode slowly northward along one of the main trading routes. After leaving Egypt, the caravan began to pass large stone fortresses occupied by the Crusaders. A truce had been signed between Saladin and Raymond of Tripoli. Therefore, the travelers expected to be left in peace. They passed the large castle at Montreal without incident. Then they approached the fortress of Kerak, near the Dead Sea, in present-day Jordan. Its high stone walls and massive towers had been built in 1142 by the Crusader knight Payen le Bouteiller. He had also controlled Montreal. The Crusaders collected tolls from all the traders who passed beneath Kerak.

In 1187, Kerak was controlled by one of the most widely feared Crusaders, Reynald of Chatillon. Reynald was a close ally of Guy of Lusignan. He had come to the Holy Land in 1148 on a Crusade against the Muslims.

Soon afterward Reynald married Constance, princess of Antioch. Reynald then ruled over this city located north of the kingdom of Jerusalem. In 1156, Reynald decided to invade the island of Cyprus, controlled by the Byzantine Empire. He tried to obtain money for the invasion from the church in Antioch. The church leader, the patriarch of Antioch, refused to give him any support. Reynald had the patriarch tortured and covered his bloody wounds with honey. Then Reynald set the patriarch outside where bees and other insects began to sting him. Finally, the patriarch agreed to give Reynald the money he needed. During the invasion of Cyprus, Reynald killed many innocent women and children.[1]

In 1162, Reynald led a raiding party against the Muslims who captured him in battle. He was imprisoned in Aleppo for the next fourteen years. Finally, the Muslims freed Reynald, after the Crusaders paid a huge ransom for his release. During this period, it was common for wealthy knights to be held for large ransoms. While Reynald was in captivity, his wife had died so he no longer had the right to rule Antioch. He married a widow named Stephanie, whose husband had controlled the castle at Kerak.

According to historian James Reston, Jr., "after his years in the dank dungeon of the Aleppo citadel he [Reynald] emerged in the grip of an even more passionate hatred of Muslims. . . ."[2] In 1182–1183, Reynald had constructed a fleet of galley ships on the Red Sea. His men sailed up and down the coastline attacking Muslim towns and killing villagers. Reynald also threatened to attack Mecca and Medina, the holy cities of Islam. Eventually, his force was defeated by the Muslims, led by Saladin's brother al-Adil. Most of Reynald's men were killed or imprisoned. Reynald escaped and fled back to Kerak. For Reynald's attempt to attack the sacred cities of Mecca and Medina, Saladin swore revenge on him.

In 1187, Reynald sent his men to attack the Muslim caravan en route from Cairo to Damascus. His soldiers rode out of Kerak, killed some of the travelers, and stole their goods. The rest of the caravan was imprisoned in Kerak. Among them was Saladin's sister. Reynald had violated the terms of the truce agreement between Saladin and Raymond of Tripoli. When Saladin received word of Reynald's attack, he immediately sent the lord of Kerak a letter. "Return what you have taken," Saladin demanded. When Reynald refused Saladin wrote to Guy of Lusignan, king of Jerusalem. Guy also asked Reynald to abide by the truce. But, once again, he refused. Referring to Saladin, Reynald said, "Just as he is the lord of his land, I am the lord of my land. I have no truce with the Arabs."[3]

WAR BEGINS BETWEEN MUSLIMS AND CRUSADERS

Since Reynald had refused to honor the truce, Saladin decided that he need no longer abide by it. Near his capital in Damascus, Saladin gathered a large army. The Muslim force included about twenty thousand soldiers.

The Muslim army marched east from Damascus at about twenty miles per day. Raymond of Tripoli feared that Saladin would strike Tiberias. This city was located

SALADIN'S ARMY

The backbone of Saladin's army was its cavalry. The light cavalry wore armor of heavily padded cotton to protect their bodies. On their heads they wore metal helmets. Their primary weapon was a bow and arrow, although some fought with crossbows. According to historian David Nicolle, the light cavalry were trained to "shoot on the move, but they normally shot while their horses stood still, drawn up in disciplined ranks. A fully trained man was expected to loose a handful of up to five arrows in two and a half seconds."

Mounted archers aimed for the horses of the Crusaders as they charged forward. "An enemy horseman approaching at [about twenty miles per hour] would therefore face five arrows during the final 30 yards of his charge."[4] The best known horse archers were the mamluks—former Muslim slaves. They had been raised to be loyal to the sultan. Fighting in cooperation with the light cavalry was the Muslim heavy cavalry. They generally wore armored mail hauberks and carried long lances as well as double-edged swords.

As Saladin's army moved out of Damascus, a screen of scouts rode in front of it. The scouts could warn Saladin, in case the enemy approached. At night the army made their camp in a circle. Saladin's tent was in the middle. "Either a trench would be dug around the camp," according to Nicolle, "or spiked 'crow's feet' [spikes] would be scattered to hamper an enemy attack."[5] Infantry accompanied the cavalry. But they played a much greater role in sieges than they did on the battlefield. They carried swords, knives, javelins, crossbows, and battle-axes. They wore mail armor and protected themselves with round leather or wooden shields.

near the Sea of Galilee. The Muslim army could easily overwhelm the city. Then the Muslims could lay siege to the castle outside Tiberias. Instead of a battle, Saladin tried a different approach—one designed to split the Crusaders. Saladin asked Raymond to allow the Muslim army to pass through Tiberias. Saladin realized that Raymond did not want war because he had signed the earlier truce with the Muslims. But he also knew that if Raymond agreed to Saladin's request, he might be seen by the other Crusaders as a traitor to their cause.

Raymond hoped to avoid a full-scale war. Therefore, he permitted an advance force from Saladin's army to pass through Tiberias. This force was led by Saladin's oldest son, al-Afdal. Al-Afdal commanded an army of several thousand troops. He advanced toward Cresson, located near Nazareth in present-day Israel. Gerard of Ridefort, master of the Knights Templar, gathered a small army to stop the Muslims. Leading about one hundred forty knights and infantry, he rode out toward Cresson.

As the Crusaders approached Cresson on May 1, they disagreed over their strategy. Some knights were opposed to attacking the Muslims, who greatly outnumbered them. Gerard called them cowards.[6] Although outnumbered, he decided to lead the Templars in an attack on al-Afdal's forces. The knights rode so quickly that they opened up a large gap between themselves and the infantry. The Muslim archers cut down most of the charging knights. Then they advanced and killed the Christian foot soldiers. Only Gerard and a few of his men were able to escape from the battlefield.

Saladin's cavalry was much quicker than the Crusader cavalry. This was due to their lighter armor.

When Raymond of Tripoli heard about the Crusader defeat at Cresson, he felt very badly. By allowing Saladin to send his son through Tiberias, Raymond had enabled him to reach Cresson and defeat the Crusaders. Raymond wanted to make up for this mistake. Therefore, he agreed to go to Jerusalem to give his support to Guy of Lusignan. Raymond also planned to join the Crusaders in a war against the Muslims.[7]

SALADIN LEADS A JIHAD

After the victory at Cresson, al-Afdal sent a letter to his father describing the Muslim victory. Saladin believed that the time had come to follow up the victory with an invasion of the Crusader kingdoms. Many of his advisors were not so sure. They believed that sending small raiding parties into Crusader territory was much safer. Saladin disagreed with them. "We must confront all the enemy's forces with all the forces of Islam," he said. "So it is foolish to disperse this concentration of troops without striking a tremendous blow in the Holy War [jihad]."[8] According to his biographer and close friend Baha al-Din:

> Saladin was very diligent in and zealous for the Jihad. . . . The Jihad, his love and passion for it, had taken mighty hold on his heart and all his being, so much so that he talked of nothing else, thought of nothing but the means to pursue it, was concerned only with its manpower and had a fondness only for those who spoke of it and encouraged it.[9]

Meanwhile, a Crusader army had begun to gather at La Safouri, west of Tiberias. Approximately twelve hundred knights and twelve thousand infantry were under the command of Guy of Lusignan. To assemble so large an army, Guy had been forced to strip most of the Crusader fortresses. He needed to call out most of their defenders to put the army into the field against Saladin. On July 1, during the heat of the summer, Saladin's forces marched eastward from the Jordan River. According to the Muslim historian Imad al-Din, "They swept like a cloud over the face of the earth, making the dust fly up . . . and sending the crows, to escape the dust, flying as far as [the stars]."[10]

At first, the Muslims bypassed Tiberias and headed toward La Safouri. After making camp, Saladin decided to lead some of his troops back to Tiberias and take the city. He easily conquered Tiberias, and began besieging the castle there. This large fortress was defended by Countess Eschiva, the wife of Raymond of Tripoli.

Countess Eschiva sent a message to her husband asking for his help at Tiberias. The messenger reached Raymond at Zippori where he had joined the forces commanded by Guy of Lusignan. Although his wife was under attack, Raymond advised Guy not to march toward Tiberias. He believed that the hot weather would force the Muslims to call off their attack. "When they depart," Raymond said, "we shall be ready and shall pounce on [Saladin's] rear guard. We shall inflict so great a loss on him that, if it please God, we and the kingdom of Jerusalem will remain in peace."[11]

According to historian James Reston, Raymond was strongly opposed by Reynald of Chatillon. Reynald believed that Raymond was a traitor who supported the Muslims. Reynald advised King Guy to attack the Muslims. Reynald was supported by Gerard de Ridefort, Master of the Templars, who thought that it was cowardly not to strike the Muslims. Guy knew that it was risky to attack Saladin, but he could not afford to be accused of cowardice. Medieval kings had to be brave in battle in order to maintain the support of the nobility. On July 3, Guy led his army out of La Safouri, across the dry plains toward Tiberias.[12]

At Hattin, masses of Crusader and Muslim soldiers met in fierce battle. This illustration of the battle appeared in a medieval manuscript.

THE BATTLE OF HATTIN

Saladin's scouts reported on the movements of the Crusader army. They told him that Guy had traveled about six miles in half a day, reaching the village of Turan. An oasis at the village provided water for the Crusaders and their horses. Guy could have remained there, where his soldiers had water. But he decided to keep marching onward. By this time, Saladin's light cavalry had come in behind the Crusaders. Therefore, they could not return to Turan. Raymond, leading the Hospitallers, hoped to reach Hattin—another source of water. But in front of him was most of Saladin's army. Instead, the Crusaders were forced to make camp at the end of the day in the dry plain, without any water.

According to Ernoul, a medieval Christian historian:

> As soon as they were encamped, Saladin ordered all his men to collect brushwood, dry grass, stubble and anything else with which they could light fires, and make barriers . . . all round the Christians. They soon did this, and the fires burned vigorously and the smoke from the fires was great; and this, together with the heat of the sun above them caused [the Crusaders] discomfort and great harm. Saladin had commanded caravans of camels loaded with water from the Sea of Tiberias to be brought up and had water pots placed near the camp. The water pots were then emptied in view of the Christians so that they should have still greater anguish through thirst, and their mounts too.[13]

The next morning, July 4, 1187, Saladin continued his strategy. His men lit fires and shot arrows through the smoke, killing the Crusaders. According to the Muslim historian Ibn al-Athir:

> The Muslim archers sent up clouds of arrows like thick swarms of locusts, killing many of the Frankish horses. The Franks, surrounding themselves with their infantry, tried to fight their way toward [the Sea of Galilee] in the hope of reaching water, but Saladin realized their objective and forestalled them by planting himself and his army in the way. He himself rode up and down the Muslim lines encouraging and restraining his troops where necessary.[14]

The Christian infantry tried to reach two hills, called the Horns of Hattin. Meanwhile, Saladin ordered his troops to attack the Crusader cavalry. The knights fought

AL-AFDAL'S ACCOUNT OF THE BATTLE OF HATTIN

Al-Afdal fought alongside his father at the Battle of Hattin and wrote an account of the fighting:

> When I saw the Franks retreating before the Moslems [sic] I cried out for joy: "We have beaten them!" But they returned to the charge with redoubled ardor and drove our army back towards my father. His response was the same as before [another charge] and the Franks retired back to the hill. Again I cried: "We have beaten them!" but my father turned to me and said: "Be silent; we shall not have beaten them until that tent falls!" As he spoke the royal tent [of King Guy] fell and the Sultan dismounted and prostrated himself in thanks to God, weeping for joy.[15]

furiously, charging repeatedly against the Muslim cavalry. But they were eventually cut to pieces by the over-whelming Muslim forces. Only Raymond and a few of his men escaped. Saladin's troops forced the Crusader infantry to surrender. He captured King Guy as well as Reynald of Chatillon. In addition, the Muslims captured a piece of the True Cross, on which Jesus Christ was believed to have been crucified. The Crusaders had carried this relic into battle inside a gold box covered with jewels.

Following the victory at Hattin, Saladin ordered some of his soldiers to bring King Guy and Reynald of Chatillon to his tent. Saladin brought water for King Guy. This was an indication that the sultan was planning to save the king's life. King Guy immediately offered some of the water to Reynald of Chatillon. "You did not ask my permission to give him water," Saladin said. "Therefore, I am not obliged to grant him mercy." Saladin was angry at Reynald for violating the truce. "How many times have you sworn an oath and then violated it," he said. Saladin had no intention of saving Reynald's life unless he agreed to become a Muslim. When Reynald refused, Saladin cut off the Crusader's arm with his sword. Then, he ordered the mamluks to cut off Reynald's head.[16]

Most of the other knights captured at Hattin were not killed. They were sold back to their families for a high ransom. Nevertheless, the Templars and Hospitallers who were caught were not ransomed. Saladin regarded them as enemies who would never live at peace with the Muslims and were dedicated to destroying them. "And so,"

Saladin accepts the surrender of Guy De Lusignan and
Reynaud De Chatillon after the Battle of Hattin.

SALADIN'S MANY ROLES

Saladin was more than a military leader. As sultan, he also had the responsibility of caring for his people. Saladin used much of the money he received as Sultan to set up colleges and hospitals. He had to supervise the economy of his empire, enact laws, and make legal decisions. Saladin showed no favoritism for members of his own family. A man from Damascus brought a case against Saladin's nephew, Taqi al-Din. The sultan hauled his nephew into court. Only after listening to two witnesses did the sultan free Taqi al-Din to leave the courtroom.

In another case, an elderly man came into court with a complaint against Saladin. The sultan then encouraged the man to speak. After the man had presented his case, Saladin called his own witnesses. They supported the sultan's position, and he dismissed the case. Saladin believed that he did not occupy such an exalted position that he could ignore the claims of his own subjects.

according to historian James Reston, "in a singular blot on his record of generosity, Saladin executed them all."[17]

THE FRUITS OF VICTORY

After his victory at Hattin, Saladin led his army against many other cities in the Crusader kingdoms. Among these was Tiberias, where Raymond's wife was defending the citadel. Saladin "granted her a safe-conduct," according to Muslim historian Imad al-Din, "for the journey for her companions and property, and she left with her women and men and luggage, taking everything to Tripoli. . . ."[18]

Since the defenders of many cities had been killed or captured at Hattin, most of them fell easily. The Muslims took the major cities of Acre, Beirut, Jaffa, Sidon, and Ascalon. Only Tyre, located along the coast, held out against a Muslim siege. The defense of the city was led by Conrad, Marquis of Montferrat. A Crusader knight, he had been living in Byzantium and came south to join the Crusade. As he reached Acre, Conrad realized that it had been captured by the Muslims. Therefore, he continued

THE ATTACK ON TYRE

According to Muslim historian Ibn al-Athir,

Tyre was like a hand stretched out into the sea, with an arm joining it to the mainland but with sea all around it. The attackers could only advance along that arm of land. The Muslims mounted an attack with catapults. . . . Saladin's own family took their turn in the battle: his son al-Afdal, his other son al-Zahir Ghazi, his brother al-Adil ibn Ayyub, his nephew Taki ad-Din [Taqi al-Din]. . . . The Franks had galleys and fire-ships with which they held the sea on either side of the isthmus along which the Muslims were attacking the city. They attacked the Muslim flanks . . . which was a grave disadvantage to our armies, who were being attacked in front by the citizens and on either side by the soldiers posted on the galleys. The isthmus was so narrow that their arrows crossed from one side to the other. Many Muslims were wounded and killed, but they failed to gain the fort.[19]

northward to Tyre. Once he arrived there, the defenders asked him to take over the defense of the city.

Saladin met with his generals. They advised him to call off the siege because winter was approaching. Instead of spending time trying to capture Tyre, Saladin decided to leave the city. He headed eastward toward Jerusalem. As Muslim historian Ibn Al-Athir put it, "It was a habit of his to tire of a siege when a town put up a firm resistance, and to move on."[20]

Jerusalem fell to Saladin on October 2, 1187, after a short siege. The victory at Hattin had led to the collapse of most of the Crusader strongholds. Saladin had achieved almost total victory over them and recaptured most of Palestine.

THE THIRD CRUSADE

THE FALL OF JERUSALEM STUNNED EUROPE. AS Saladin's conquests continued, the leaders of western Europe assembled the Third Crusade. They hoped that this crusade would defeat the Muslims.

In November 1187, Saladin returned to Tyre to lay siege to the city once again. He was accompanied by his brother al-Adil and son al-Afdal. Many of the Christians who had left Jerusalem after its capture had fled to Tyre. They were put to work improving the city's defenses by Conrad of Montferrat, who was still in command of the city. Saladin's siege was no more successful than the earlier one and he was forced to retreat early in 1188.

Nevertheless, Saladin had more success against other Crusader strongholds. Instead of always using raw power to conquer a city, he often resorted to other means. These methods were illustrated at the siege of Bourzey Castle in 1188. As historian Mark T. Abate wrote, "To draw attention and defenders away from the weakest point in

CONRAD OF MONTFERRAT

Conrad was born about 1146 in Montferrat, located in northern Italy. He was educated at the court of his father, William III of Montferrat. William left Montferrat and became a crusader in the Kingdom of Jerusalem. Conrad hoped to join him in 1187. About that time, the Kingdom of Jerusalem fell to Saladin, and William was captured. Conrad tried to enter Acre, which had been captured by the Muslims. But instead he went north to Tyre.

During the first siege in 1187, Saladin brought William in front of the gates of Tyre. The sultan announced that he planned to execute William unless he persuaded his son to surrender the city. Instead, William called on Conrad to keep fighting. Although William had not cooperated with the Muslims, Saladin released him. Tyre held out, and the Muslims retreated. When Saladin returned in November, he tried to cut off Tyre by land and sea. He placed an Egyptian naval squadron in the harbor. However, Conrad led a daring night raid on December 30, 1187. The raid destroyed many of the Egyptian galleys. Soon afterward, Saladin decided to call off the siege. His closest advisers told him, "we have been here for a long time and our target is out of reach. Our men have been killed and wounded and our funds are running low."[1]

Conrad later married Isabella, the daughter of King Almaric. During the early 1190s, Conrad and Isabella became the king and queen of Jerusalem. But Conrad was murdered in 1192 and never carried out his duties as king.

the castle's defenses, Saladin assembled a mass of troops on the opposite and much stronger side. The ruse [trick] worked when the surprise attack struck at the true target. Bourzey was taken and at little cost." Indeed, Saladin had used similar tactics at Tyre in 1187. The city was on the point of surrender until Conrad appeared and rallied the defenders.[2]

THE RELEASE OF A CRUSADER

Later in 1188, Saladin decided to free Guy of Lusignan. He had been captured at the Battle of Hattin. Guy's wife, Sybilla, had made a special request to Saladin to free her husband. Saladin may have also hoped that by freeing Guy he might cause trouble for Conrad at Tyre.[3] These two men did not get along with each other. Each one believed that he should be in charge of the Crusader forces.

As a condition of his release, Guy promised Saladin not to become involved in any new campaigns against the Muslims. However, Guy immediately broke his promise. He journeyed to Tyre and began raising a new army. As Saladin had guessed, conflict broke out between Guy and Conrad. Guy demanded to be put in charge of the defenses at Tyre since he was the king of Jerusalem. Conrad replied that Guy had lost his right to be king because of his defeat at Hattin. He had also been captured by Saladin. In addition, Jerusalem had been lost to the Crusaders while Guy was king.

Nevertheless, Guy continued to raise an army outside of Tyre. Meanwhile, Saladin was busy capturing additional

Crusader fortresses. In the south, Saladin's brother, al-Adil, laid siege to the large citadel of Kerak. Although the siege took many months, the castle finally fell to the Muslims.

THE SIEGE OF ACRE

By 1189, Guy had gathered an army of approximately ten thousand troops around Tyre. With this new force, he marched northward toward Acre, which was controlled by the Muslims. Acre lay on the coast of the Mediterranean. Two sides of the city were along the water. Acre's harbor was guarded by a forty-foot tower, called the Tower of Flies. The other two sides lay on a broad plain. On one corner of the walls was another tower, called the Accursed Tower. For his betrayal of Jesus Christ, Judas Iscariot received thirty pieces of silver that were made at the site of the tower.

Saladin had received information about Guy's march toward Acre. The sultan wanted to attack the Crusaders along the way before they ever reached the city. "If the Franks reach their destination," he said, "and get a firm hold of the territory, it will not be easy for us to dislodge and overcome them. It is better to attack before they reach Acre."[4] Saladin's generals disagreed with this strategy. "Let them take up their position before Acre and we shall cut them to pieces in one day," one of them said.[5]

Guy's army arrived at Acre on August 29. They immediately began to dig trenches around the city for a siege. Guy was supported by a fleet made up of Danish galleys that had joined the Crusade. Guy began to attack

In the battles that Saladin's soldiers won, they often succeeded in surrounding the Crusaders.

Acre in early September. The attack was called off when Guy received reports that Saladin was marching to relieve the city. Once Saladin's forces arrived, battles broke out with the Crusader army. The Crusaders lay between the Muslim forces and the city of Acre. According to Muslim historian Al-Athir, in early September, Saladin's nephew Taqi al-Din

> led a terrible charge against the enemy facing him on the right wing and dislodged them from their

position. They fell over one another in their retreat, not pausing even to help a brother in their flight to safety with near-by companies. . . . Immediately Taqi ad-Din occupied the area they had abandoned and made contact with the city. The Muslims were able to go in and out, communications were established and the blockade of the inhabitants was broken.[6]

In early October, another fierce clash broke out as the Crusaders tried to regain the advantage. Saladin commanded the center of the Muslim forces along with his sons, al-Afdal and az-Zahir. The Crusaders attacked with their crossbowmen and infantry, driving back the Muslims. According to historians Malcolm Lyons and D.E.P. Jackson, the Crusaders pushed through the Muslim center. Many soldiers ran from the battlefield. In fact, some "did not halt until they were safely . . . at Damascus itself."[7] Saladin brought in fresh troops and stopped the retreat. They were joined by about five thousand Muslim troops who attacked from inside Acre. Yelling "On, on for Islam," Saladin led his men in an assault against the Crusaders. They were driven back inside their lines. Lyons and Jackson wrote that Crusader losses were about seven thousand troops "and the corpses were thrown into the river [Belus, located near Acre] to pollute the water," so the Crusader army could not drink it.[8]

Saladin wanted to continue the attack and wipe out Guy's army. However, his generals said the Muslim soldiers were too tired. Instead of attacking the Crusaders, Saladin's generals advised him that it was better to wait for reinforcements from Egypt.[9] Indeed, Saladin relied heavily on Egyptian soldiers and ships to carry on the siege of Acre. In November, ships from Egypt arrived under the command of Emir Lu'lu. They brought more siege weapons and infantry. Saladin also brought in food supplies from Egypt to feed the defenders of Acre.

By the end of 1189, Saladin's army still remained outside Acre. The Crusaders lay in between the Muslims and the city itself, attacking the walls of Acre. The Muslim historian Baha al-Din wrote that the Crusaders

> constructed three towers of wood and iron. . . . They were mounted on wheels and each one could accommodate more than 500 men. . . . Their flat tops were large enough for a [catapult] to be set up there. This worked on the minds of the Muslims and filled them with fear for the city, more than can be expressed.[10]

But a young Muslim metalworker figured out a way to destroy the towers. From inside the city, he filled pots with naphtha. These pots were hurled at the towers and covered them with naphtha. Then, he directed the catapults to hurl naphtha-filled pots that had been set on fire. These struck the towers, "and the whole became like a huge mountain of fire, whose tongues of flame rose into the sky."[11] Many Crusaders were burned to death.

During the siege, the Crusaders also tried to batter down a gate at Acre with a huge battering ram. The ram contained a massive metal head. Once again, the defenders resorted to naphtha to burn the ram. Then they brought what was left of it inside the city.

BETWEEN THE LINES

When the Muslims and Christians were not fighting, they called a truce. During the truce, they sometimes met each other between the lines and enjoyed entertainment together. They sang songs and even held wrestling matches. Meanwhile, some Muslims used the truce to enrich themselves. They snuck into the Crusader camp to steal equipment and carry off innocent women and children.

One three-month-old child was taken from his mother. Then he was brought to the marketplace and sold into slavery. The mother was so upset that she told several Muslim leaders what had happened. They gave her permission to take her story to Saladin. "After he had asked about her case," Baha al-Din reported:

> and it had been explained, he had compassion for her and, with tears in his eyes, he ordered the infant to be brought to him. People went and found that it had been sold in the market. The sultan ordered the purchase price to be paid to the purchaser and the child taken from him. He himself stayed where he had halted until the infant was produced and then handed over to the woman who took it, wept mightily, and hugged it to her bosom, while people watched her and wept also.[12]

Saladin tried to coordinate his assaults on the Crusaders with attacks by the defenders of Acre. To send messages into the city, Saladin used carrier pigeons. As one Arab historian put it, "These birds kept secrets loyally. They ensured the flow of information, guarded the letters jealously, showed themselves as generous as the best of noblemen. They braved dangers, never made a mistake, and were prized as precious possessions."[13]

Saladin also relied on Muslim swimmers. They jumped into the water outside Acre. Then they dove beneath the Christian galleys and reached the walls of the city. The

ISA THE SWIMMER

In his biography of Saladin, Baha al-Din told the story of one swimmer. His name was Isa, Arabic for Jesus. He carried money into Acre in his belt, tied around him as he swam:

> One night, carrying three purses . . . and messages for the army in his belt he set out on his swim, but met with an accident from which he died. It was some time before we learnt of his death. It was his custom, on entering the city, to send up a messenger-pigeon to tell of his arrival. When the bird did not appear we realized that he must be dead. One day some time later a group of people was on the beach by the city when the sea cast up a body on the shore. Examination revealed that it was Isa the swimmer. In his belt they found the gold and the wax-paper containing the letters. . . .[14]

swimmers brought money to pay the Muslim troops, and messages from Saladin to the commanders of Acre. When the swimmers returned from Acre, they often carried messages with them for Saladin.

Meanwhile, Saladin succeeded in getting in a few supplies by ship. On one occasion, Muslim sailors disguised themselves as Christians and flew Christian banners on their galley. When stopped by the Crusader blockade, they pretended to be part of a Christian naval force. The Crusaders let them pass. The Muslims entered the harbor at Acre with supplies. But these were far from enough to feed all the defenders. The Crusader blockade had become far too strong for Saladin to send in Egyptian supply ships. As a result, the siege became a stalemate between Muslims and Crusaders. It lasted for two years.

OPENING THE THIRD CRUSADE

While the struggle continued in Palestine, a new crusade had begun in western Europe. Following the fall of Jerusalem in 1187, Josias, Bishop of Tyre, left Palestine. He brought word of the defeat to Europe. In Rome, Pope Gregory VIII called on Christian leaders to mount a new crusade. It was known as the Third Crusade. The Crusader armies were led by Richard the Lionheart, king of England; Philip Augustus, king of France; and Frederick Barbarossa, emperor of Germany.

In July 1190, Richard met with Philip Augustus at Vezelay in France. To raise a Crusader army, Henry II had levied the "Saladin tithe" in England. Each person was required to pay 10 percent of his income. With this money, Richard put together a large army to fight the Muslims. It included mounted knights, archers, crossbowmen, and infantry. Some of his soldiers were mercenaries. That is, they were hired from other areas of Europe to participate in the Crusade. Dressed in armor and covered with a white smock bearing a red cross, Richard met with Philip Augustus. Both men knew each other from years of campaigning in France. Philip planned to lead his army to Genoa, located in northern Italy. Then he intended to travel across the Mediterranean to Palestine.

Richard intended to march south to Marseilles, on the French coast. There he expected the English navy to join him. The English ships were galleys, manned by rowers, with sails that could take advantage of the wind. They

THE SALADIN TITHE, 1188

The Saladin Tax was called a tithe, meaning a tenth, because each person was required to give 10 percent of his or her income to the king. According to the tithe:

> Each person will give in charity one tenth of his rents and movable goods for the taking of the land of Jerusalem; except for the arms, horses, and clothing of knights, and likewise for the horses, books, clothing, and vestments, and church furniture of the clergy, and except for precious stones [jewels] belonging to the clergy or the laity. . . . But the clergy and knights who have taken the cross, shall give none of that tithe except from their own goods and the property of their lord. . . . [15]

RICHARD I, THE LIONHEART

Born in 1157, Richard was the son of Henry II, king of England, and Eleanor of Aquitaine. Richard grew up at Poitiers in his mother's duchy of Aquitaine, located in southern France. Poitiers was considered a major center of literature and music in western Europe. Poets composed poems of love between knights and ladies. Minstrels wrote songs about courageous knights who defended Christianity in the Crusades.

As a young man, Richard seemed to exemplify the ideal medieval knight. He was tall, athletic, and handsome, with blond hair. Richard was also an experienced military leader. During the 1170s, he battled nobles in Aquitaine who rebelled against his parents' rule. Richard laid siege to their castles, forcing them to surrender. In addition to Aquitaine, his father, King Henry, claimed other lands in France. When revolts broke out among French nobles who refused to recognize Henry as their king, Richard put down the rebellions. Sometimes he resorted to burning villages. He also killed innocent peasant farmers and destroyed their fields. These brutal tactics were designed to starve the nobles and their castles into surrender. In 1189, following the death of Henry II, Richard became king of England.

sailed from the coast of western Europe. Their course took them southward in the Atlantic Ocean. They traveled as far as southern Spain, and then into the Mediterranean Sea toward southern France. The English army reached Marseilles ahead of the ships, which had been delayed by a storm at sea. When the navy did not appear after several days, Richard left the army in Marseilles. With a few troops, he headed toward Italy. Eventually, Richard arrived in southern Italy and traveled to Messina, Sicily. There the English fleet, led by Robert de Sable, finally arrived. The ships carried Richard's army. In the meantime, Philip Augustus had also reached Sicily along with his army.

SICILY AND CYPRUS

Sicily was ruled by King Tancred, no friend of Richard the Lionheart. Tancred had taken control of the kingdom, after the death of the previous king. He had also imprisoned the king's widow, Sicily's Queen Joanna Plantagenet. Joanna was Richard's sister. According to Richard of Devizes, King Richard asked that Joanna be released and her dowry returned. Usually, a noble woman brought money and other expensive possessions with her to seal a marriage to a noble lord. Joanna's dowry included a golden chair. It also included "a golden table 12 feet long, a silken tent, a hundred first-class galleys with everything necessary for them for two years . . . twenty-four golden cups, and 24 golden plates."[16]

Faced with a powerful Crusader army, Tancred released Joanna. But he kept most of her possessions. Richard

SALADIN AND FREDERICK BARBAROSSA

While Richard and Philip Augustus were preparing to travel to Palestine, an invasion of Syria had already been launched. It was led by Frederick Barbarossa, the German emperor. In 1188, the king gathered an army, numbering approximately fifteen thousand troops. He prepared to head south through Hungary and Turkey into Syria. When Saladin learned that Barbarossa was gathering an army of Crusaders, he moved northward. His plan was to capture the few remaining Crusader strongholds in northern Syria. As a result, Barbarossa's troops would find their march threatened by Muslim fortresses. These citadels had fallen to the Muslims in 1188.

In 1189, Barbarossa led his army southward past Constantinople and into Turkey. Saladin received constant reports of the German leader's progress from the Byzantine emperor, Isaac. The sultan had formed an alliance with Isaac. He feared that the German crusaders might try to take over some of his territory. By 1190, Frederick had reached the river Goksu, on the way to Antioch. He was told the river was too swift to cross safely. Frederick jumped in anyway, thinking he could swim across. He was swept away by the current and drowned. Without a leader, most of his soldiers returned to Germany. But a small number of troops marched southward to Acre under the command of Leopold, duke of Austria. Nevertheless, the threat to Saladin from the German crusaders had ended.

decided to teach Tancred a lesson. Historian James Reston also believed that King Richard wanted to give his knights some combat experience before they reached Palestine. Consequently, fighting soon broke out between Tancred's soldiers and King Richard's troops.[17] After defeating Tancred, Richard's troops left Sicily on April 10, 1191.

On route southward toward Palestine, Richard's fleet again encountered fierce storms. One of the ships carried the king's fiancée, Berengaria, a Spanish princess. She had been brought to Sicily by Richard's mother, Eleanor of Aquitaine. Eleanor wanted the couple to marry so they could produce an heir to the English throne. The ship carrying Berengaria was driven toward the coast of Cyprus, an island in the Mediterranean. Eventually, Berengaria was joined by Richard and the rest of the English fleet. But one of the ships, carrying a large quantity of money to finance the Third Crusade, had been wrecked. Richard's treasure was seized by Isaac Comnenus, the king of Cyprus. The king refused to return it to Richard.

Richard wanted to regain his treasure. He also recognized that Cyprus was a rich agricultural area that could supply wheat for his troops in Palestine. Therefore, he undertook a campaign to take over the island. Richard began by attacking Limassol, a city located on the coast of Cyprus. Isaac tried to defend Limassol, but it was captured by the Crusaders. Nevertheless, they were unable to capture the king, who fled inland with some of his troops. Richard pursued him and defeated Isaac's forces, but once again the king disappeared. However, Isaac was unable to

Frederick Barbarossa of Germany (with feet on shield) was dragged from the river Goksu after he had drowned. His body was then readied for burial.

carry off Richard's treasure, which was recaptured by the English king.[18]

Soon afterward, King Richard was joined in Cyprus by Guy of Lusignan and some of his knights. Guy informed Richard of the desperate situation at Acre. The Crusaders were running short of food and had been forced to kill some of their own horses to survive. Malaria, a fatal disease carried by mosquitoes, was killing off some of the Crusaders. In fact, Guy's wife, Sybilla, and his daughters had already died. That meant that Guy no longer had a legal claim to be king of Jerusalem. Guy asked for Richard's help against Conrad. He informed Richard that King Philip had already arrived in Acre with his army. Philip gave his support to Conrad, who was claiming the throne of Jerusalem through his wife Isabella. She was the daughter of King Almaric and the half sister of Guy's deceased wife Sybilla.

Richard and Guy pledged to help each other. Guy's knights immediately joined Richard's attack on Isaac Comnenus. After most of his castles fell to the Crusaders, Isaac Comnenus was finally captured and imprisoned. After defeating Isaac, Richard married Berrengia, who became queen of England. Shortly afterward, he left her in Cyprus and sailed to Palestine. Richard arrived at Acre in June 1191, several weeks behind Philip and his army. There the Crusaders faced Sultan Saladin.

SALADIN AND RICHARD I

THE SIEGE OF ACRE AND THE BATTLE OF ARSUF marked a turning point in the warfare between Muslims and Crusaders. Saladin and Richard the Lionheart matched each other as battlefield commanders. The result was a standoff between their two armies.

Saladin had put the defense of Acre into the hands of two of his most experienced commanders, Karakush and Mashtub. Emir Karakush was a former slave of the sultan, who had helped construct the defenses at Cairo, Egypt. Emir Mashtub, who was the commanding general at Acre, was a Kurd, like Saladin himself. Both men tried to rally their forces and hold out against the Crusaders. But the task of defending Acre became more and more difficult. Richard was especially respected and feared by the Muslims. As Baha al-Din put it, "He was wise and experienced in warfare and his coming had a dread and frightening effect on the hearts of the Muslims."[1]

Led by King Richard and Philip Augustus, the Crusaders brought their siege engines in front of the walls of Acre. Their soldiers constructed a huge tower with a catapult on top of it. Other catapults were brought up before the Accursed Tower. According to one report, the Crusaders put three hundred catapults to work against Acre's walls. Richard had brought huge granite stones from Sicily. These stones were heavier than the limestone rocks of Palestine.[2] As a result, they could do far more damage when hurled against the walls of the city. Meanwhile, engineers and miners were at work, digging tunnels underneath the walls of Acre. At one point, Christian miners encountered Muslims tunneling from inside the city. A deadly fight broke out under the walls.

ACRE

Richard of Devizes described the siege this way:

> . . . the bowmen on it [the huge tower] kept up an unceasing rain of arrows on the Turks. . . . The stone-throwers, skillfully placed, broke down the walls by repeated shots. . . . The king himself ran about through the ranks, ordering, exhorting, and inspiring, and he was thus everywhere beside each man, so that to him alone might be ascribed what each man did.[3]

By July the walls around the Accursed Tower were falling down under a tremendous assault by the Crusaders. Meanwhile, Richard had been stricken by a serious illness. Historian James Reston wrote that it was probably scurvy, a disease caused by a lack of vitamin C. Nevertheless,

Richard did not stay in his bed. He ordered his men to bring him to the battlefield where he supervised the efforts to take Acre. In fact, Richard carried his own crossbow. He used it to shoot down Muslims from the walls of Acre.[4]

Meanwhile, Saladin continued launching attacks against the Crusader trenches around Acre. He urged the defenders inside the city to hold out and promised that more supplies would soon be arriving. But a Muslim supply ship was captured by the Crusader galleys in early July. Problems were also growing inside the Muslim ranks. Saladin's own troops had grown weary of the combat and wanted to stop the fighting. As Baha al-Din put it, "the army did not help him [Saladin] . . . and said: 'we are putting the whole of Islam at risk.'"[5]

Inside Acre, the situation grew more desperate daily. The Crusaders repeatedly knocked openings in the walls. They tried to launch attacks through them into Acre. Seeing no way to save the city, Mashtub and Karakush opened negotiations in early July. The Muslim commanders first approached King Philip, asking that the defenders be permitted to leave Acre in peace. Philip refused. Therefore, the Muslim leaders decided to continue fighting. Richard then agreed to offer them their lives if Saladin returned a piece of the True Cross. This was carried by the Crusaders into the Battle of Hattin and captured by the Muslims. Richard also wanted a huge sum of money and the return of many prisoners who had disappeared at Hattin in 1187.

However, the prisoners had already been sold into slavery. So Saladin hesitated in the negotiations and

SALADIN'S CALL TO VICTORY

"Where is the sense of honour of the Muslims, the pride of the believers, the zeal of the faithful?" Saladin said:

> . . . observe how far the Franks have gone; what unity they have achieved, what aims they pursue, what help they have given, what sums of money they have borrowed and spent, what wealth they have collected and distributed and divided among them! . . . In defense of their religion they consider it a small thing to spend life and soul, and they have kept their infidel brothers supplied with arms and champions for the war. . . . The Muslims, on the other hand, are weakened and demoralized. . . . This is the moment to cast off lethargy, to summon from far and near all those men who have blood in their veins.[6]

intended to continue fighting. The sultan called on his troops to attack again.

Mashtub and Karakush made further offers. Eventually, they reached an agreement with King Richard. He received a huge sum of money. In addition, the Muslims agreed to hand over more than two thousand prisoners and five hundred Christian captives.

On July 12, 1191, Acre surrendered. Saladin was stunned and saddened. As Baha al-Din wrote, "I was present in attendance on the sultan, who was more affected than a bereft mother or a distracted love-sick girl."[7] Many of the Muslims were held by King Richard and King Philip for ransom. Among them were Mashtub and Karakush. According to Richard of Devizes, well-to-do Muslims

> by swallowing many gold pieces, made purses of their bellies, for they knew in advance that whatever anyone might have of any value would be counted as an offence and would lead him, if he resisted, to the gallows and be booty for the victors. All of them therefore came out before the kings completely defenseless and with no money outside their skins and were put into safe keeping.[8]

Thinking that Saladin was refusing terms of surrender, Richard I had three thousand Muslim soldiers massacred at Acre.

The French and English Crusaders took control of the city. Leopold of Austria also claimed a part in the victory because his German knights had participated in the siege. Richard and Philip refused to share the victory with him.

Saladin had no choice but to accept the decision made by his generals. Nevertheless, he was in no hurry to carry out the terms of the surrender. Within thirty days, Saladin was expected to hand over the Christian captives. But he said that they were not ready. Richard believed that Saladin was refusing to honor the terms of the surrender. In retaliation, he brought three thousand Muslim soldiers outside the gates of Acre. He ordered his soldiers to kill all of them. "Then as one man they charged them," Baha al-Din wrote, "and with stabbings and blows with the sword they slew them in cold blood, while the Muslim advance guard watched, not knowing what to do because they were at some distance from them."[9]

THE CAMPAIGN AFTER ACRE

After the siege ended, Saladin ordered his army to retreat from Acre. Inside the city, the victorious Crusaders began to rebuild the walls that had been destroyed during the siege. They intended to turn Acre into another important stronghold, like Tyre to the north. Richard commanded the reconstruction project. King Philip, who had suffered from various illnesses during his stay in Palestine, had decided to return to France. Philip sailed to Antioch. Then he traveled on to Rome, northward through Germany, and back to his royal palace.

Richard remained the sole commander of the Crusader army. It numbered about twenty-five thousand to thirty thousand troops. These included mounted knights, Templars and Hospitallers, archers and crossbowmen. In August, the army left Acre and began heading southward. They marched along the coast. To their right, at sea, sailed the large Crusader navy. Saladin did not know where Richard intended to take his forces. The Crusader army could have been planning to strike Jerusalem. On the other hand, Richard might be intending to march as far south as the Muslim fortress of Ascalon. This great citadel guarded the northern approach to Egypt.

The Crusaders marched during the early morning, before the summer sun became too hot. The Templars led the march, with King Richard riding along with them. Guy of Lusignan commanded the center, and the Hospitallers guarded the rear of the army. Once the day became too hot, the Crusaders rested. As historian Christopher Libertini wrote,

> Anticipating the tactics of his enemy, Richard orchestrated a brilliant scheme of maneuver for his forces. To ward off harassing attacks of Saladin's cavalry, which were designed to slowly bleed the Crusader army of its horses, Richard organized his foot soldiers to guard the exposed left flank of his army [the inland side]. To the right of this protective screen marched the cream of his force, his heavy cavalry. Finally, along his right flank, which was closest to the sea, he placed his baggage train. . . .[10]

Richard marched seventy miles down the coast in about fifteen days.

Saladin's soldiers followed closely along the route of the Crusader army. Mounted archers swept down on small groups of Crusaders, firing arrows at them. Many of these arrows stuck in the quilted chest protection worn by the infantrymen and did little damage. "I saw various individuals . . . with the arrows fixed in their backs, pressing on . . . quite unconcerned," wrote Baha al-Din. "The Muslims were shooting arrows on their flanks, trying to incite them to break ranks, while they controlled themselves severely and covered the route in this way, traveling very steadily as their ships moved along at sea opposite them."[11]

The Muslims did far more damage with the arrows they aimed at the enemy horses. Hundreds of horses were killed. Saladin's son al-Afdal also attacked a group of Crusaders who had fallen behind the rest of the army. "Had we been in force, we could have taken them," he wrote his father.[12]

With approximately eighty thousand troops, Saladin greatly outnumbered the Crusader army. He had tried to break up their ranks. Saladin hoped to lure some of the mounted knights into an attack, and surround them before Richard could come to their aid with the rest of his army. But Richard's army was far too disciplined. During one attack, Richard himself was wounded while driving back the Muslims. But he continued leading his army southward.

Richard's army drew closer to Jerusalem. Saladin realized that time was running out to engage the Crusaders in a major battle. Meanwhile, Richard had opened peace negotiations with Saladin's brother al-Adil. The king had

SALADIN'S SHIPS

Muslim ships during the Middle Ages were based on designs used by Greeks and Romans in the ancient world. These ships were long galleys. The ancient ships were powered by a crew of about two hundred, most of whom manned the oars. In addition to the oars, each galley had one or two sails to take advantage of the wind in the Mediterranean Sea. When the wind was blowing in the direction that the galley wanted to travel, the oarsmen could rest. They let the sails do the work for them.

Another influence on Saladin's ships were the long boats used by the Vikings. Since the ninth century, Viking ships from Scandinavia had raided Europe. Each Viking long ship had about ninety crewmen, thirty of whom worked as oarsmen. Every ship also had a colorful square sail that could take advantage of the wind. On the long ships, one of the crew used an oar on the side to stir the boat. The Muslim galleys were somewhat different than the Viking ships.

Saladin's ships had lateen sails. These were triangular in shape. Each ship had two or three lateen sails that were powered by the wind. The galleys were about one hundred to two hundred feet long, with forty oars to move them forward. Some of the galleys had as many as one hundred forty rowers. For steering, the galleys had rudders. Each ship had archers and crossbowmen, who could attack enemy galleys at sea. In addition, the galleys had a small enclosed area at the bow and stern, called a castle. Another type of ship in Saladin's navy was the cog. This was a sailing ship with lateen sails and a castle at the prow and stern. The cogs were used primarily to transport supplies.

tried to negotiate with Saladin. But the sultan did not believe that this was the role that two leaders should play. Saladin was not convinced that the negotiations would lead anywhere. But he told his brother to continue them "until we receive the reinforcements we are expecting."[13]

THE BATTLE OF ARSUF

By early September, the Crusader army was nearing Jaffa—a key Muslim stronghold. The Crusaders moved slowly, trying to keep all of their soldiers together. In addition, they wanted to stay in sight of the galleys at sea, which provided supplies to the soldiers. Saladin decided that the time for a decisive battle was drawing closer. If the Crusaders captured Jaffa, they could easily march toward Jerusalem—just a short distance away.

Near Arsuf, north of Jaffa, the Crusaders began to approach a large orchard. To the east lay a forest, and behind it a ridge of hills. Saladin hoped to provoke the Crusader knights to charge toward the woods where they might be cut down by the Muslim archers there.

The Crusaders passed the forest of Arsuf on September 1. Suddenly, Muslim trumpets and drums sounded the call to battle. Approximately two thousand Muslim archers advanced from the forest toward the Crusaders. After the archers had inflicted some casualties, Saladin launched his knights against the enemy. The Crusader army turned from its line of march to face the Muslims, with the infantry in front. The Muslim cavalry struck at that part of the Crusader army that was occupied by the

Hospitallers. As the Muslims attacked, they encountered the enemy infantry, which withstood a terrible onslaught. Behind them were the Hospitaller knights mounted on their horses. The Hospitallers wanted to charge the Muslims. The master of the Hospitallers rode over to Richard's position. "Sire, we are sore discomforted and suffer shame and bitter pain—our horses are all being slain."[14] Richard asked him to hold back until the entire Crusader army had halted and faced the enemy. Then he planned to launch a simultaneous charge against Saladin's army. Richard expected that such a powerful attack might drive the Muslims from the field.

As the Muslim assault continued, several of the Hospitallers could not hold themselves back. Against Richard's orders, they decided to charge. As the charge began, Richard ordered the rest of his knights to join them. "I saw them grouped together in the middle of the foot-soldiers," Baha al-Din wrote. "They took their lances and gave a shout as one man. The infantry opened gaps for them and they charged in unison along their whole line. One group charged our right wing, another our left and the third our centre. Our men gave way before them. It happened that I was in the centre, which took to wholesale flight."[15] Baha al-Din hoped to find refuge in the right or left wing of the Muslim army. But a flight was under way across the entire line. The charge of the Crusader knights had taken the Muslims by surprise and beaten them. Saladin tried to rally his troops but they kept fleeing. Only a small contingent of the sultan's own Mamluks stood firm. Finally the flight stopped. "All who saw the sultan's troop holding its position with drums beating were ashamed to pass beyond it and feared the disaster that might follow, so they rallied to his troop and a large number assembled there."[16] By this time, the battle had reached the woods. The Crusaders drew back fearing that Saladin might try to ambush them if they proceeded any farther.

Arsuf was a major defeat for Saladin. The Muslim army lost an estimated seven thousand troops, about ten times

The armies of Saladin and Richard I battle at Arsuf.

as many as the Crusaders.[17] Saladin told his commanders how extremely unhappy he had been that they did not fight any harder. One of his sons, eighteen-year-old al-Malik al-Zahir had fought alongside his father at Arsuf. "Most sacred Sultan," he said:

> these words are unfair, for we fought with all our strength against the Franks. With fearless hearts and zeal we attacked them, but they are armed with armor that no weapon can pierce, and so our blows fell harmless. . . . Moreover, among their number is a leader superior to any man we have ever seen. . . . Such a king seems born to command the whole world.[18]

THE CAMPAIGN CONTINUES

After the victory at Arsuf, King Richard began leading his army south to Jaffa. Saladin ordered that the stronghold should be destroyed before the Crusaders could take control of it. Meanwhile, he tried to entice Richard into another battle. Mounted archers were sent to attack the Crusader line of march. But Richard refused to permit his knights to pursue the archers who might lead them into an ambush.

As the Crusaders reached Jaffa, Saladin decided to divide his forces. He could not determine whether the Crusaders might eventually head toward Jerusalem or south to Ascalon. He left al-Adil with one part of the army to watch the Crusaders. With the rest of the army, Saladin marched south to Ascalon. A major seaport and the

DESTRUCTION OF ASCALON

The Muslim historian Baha al-Din described the destruction of Ascalon. Saladin "summoned the governor, Qaysar, one of his senior mamlukes [sic] and one of the wisest, and ordered him to put pickaxes to work," recalled Baha al-Din:

> I saw him after he had passed through the market and the encampment personally urging the men to start the work of destruction. He assigned sections of the wall to the men. To each emir and detachment of troops he appointed a particular stretch of ... wall and a particular tower to destroy. Our men entered the town and great cries and weepings arose [from the residents]. . . . The inhabitants were sorely grieved for the town and great were their wailings and weepings on leaving their homes. They started to sell what they were unable to transport.[19]

gateway to Egypt, Ascalon could not be allowed to fall into enemy hands. Therefore, Saladin made a difficult decision. He ordered his men to destroy the fortified port so it could not be used by the Crusaders. The destruction began in mid September 1191.

With Ascalon destroyed, Saladin waited. He did not know what the Crusaders would do now. Richard established his headquarters at Jaffa. Now, would he head south or decide to attack Jerusalem?

BATTLE FOR A KINGDOM

THE BATTLES OF THE THIRD CRUSADE ENDED in 1192. During the year, the conflict centered around Jerusalem.

PEACE NEGOTIATIONS

During the fall of 1191, the Crusader army was camped at Jaffa on the coast of the Mediterranean Sea. Along with King Richard were his wife, Berengaria, and his sister Joanna. Many skirmishes occurred between the Crusaders and the Muslims. Saladin's army was only a few miles away at Ramla, located between Jaffa and Jerusalem. Richard enjoyed the challenge of combat, whether it was part of a major battle or a small skirmish. He regularly rode out from Jaffa with some of his men to engage the Muslims. Once, Richard rested in the woods during a campaign. He was almost captured by a large force of Muslim cavalry.

However, Richard rode to safety before the Muslims could surround him.

The Crusaders were only a few miles from Jerusalem. But they faced a Muslim army that far outnumbered them. Before risking another bloody battle, Richard tried negotiating over the future of Palestine. The English king sent a letter to Saladin through his brother al-Adil. It said, "I am to salute you, and tell you that the Muslims and Franks are bleeding to death, the country is utterly ruined and goods and lives have been sacrificed on both sides. The time has come to stop this."[1]

Richard demanded that the entire kingdom of Jerusalem should be restored to the Crusaders. This included the city of Jerusalem and the former Crusader strongholds along the Mediterranean coast. Richard also wanted the piece of the True Cross that had been taken by the Muslims at Hattin. But Saladin refused to consider such a proposal. "Jerusalem is ours just as much as it is yours," he wrote. "Let not the king imagine that we shall give it up, for we are unable to breathe a word of that among the Muslims. As for the land, it is also ours originally. Your conquest of it was an unexpected accident due to the weakness of the Muslims there at that time."[2]

Since Saladin had turned down Richard's first offer, he came forward with another proposal. Richard suggested that his sister, Joanna, and al-Adil, Saladin's brother, should marry. The king suggested that Joanna and al-Adil might then rule the kingdom of Jerusalem together. The territory would then be open to both Christians and Muslims. Once Joanna was informed of this proposal, however, she told the king that she was not interested in marrying a Muslim. Richard then proposed that al-Adil might become a Christian. But al-Adil showed no interest in this suggestion. Therefore, Richard then proposed that he marry the king's niece, Eleanor. But al-Adil was uninterested in marrying her.

While these negotiations were occurring, Saladin received messengers from Conrad, ruler of Tyre. Conrad had participated in the siege of Acre and considered himself the rightful king of Jerusalem. But he knew that Richard still backed Guy of Lusignan. Conrad also feared that the English king might try to take control of Tyre. Therefore, Conrad tried to make a deal with Saladin. Conrad agreed not to support Richard. In return, he wanted Saladin's help in case of an attack by the English king. Conrad also expected Saladin to give him the city of Sidon.

"Saladin explained the situation to the amirs," wrote Baha al-Din, "and asked them to reveal their hearts to him and tell him which plan . . . seemed preferable to them. . . . The counselors held that peace must be made with the King. . . ."[3] They did not trust Conrad.

THE WAR CONTINUES

Nevertheless, none of the peace offers made by King Richard were acceptable to Saladin. Therefore, he began to prepare his army for the battle to defend Jerusalem that seemed likely in the future. Saladin destroyed some of the citadels that lay between Jaffa and Jerusalem. By late

October 1191, the Crusader army was advancing from Jaffa eastward. But their march was slowed by the fall rains that turned the roads into mud. As the Crusaders marched toward Jerusalem, Muslim horsemen swooped down on their lightly defended supply lines. Richard advanced slowly until the end of 1191. The weather was growing worse. It made a long siege more and more difficult. Richard also feared that his army might be attacked from the rear by some of Saladin's forces.

Finally, Richard called off the advance. Instead of Jerusalem, he decided to head south toward Ascalon. King Richard planned to rebuild the city. He wanted Ascalon to become a major Crusader base for a possible invasion of Egypt. The French crusaders disagreed with his decision. They still wanted to attack Jerusalem. Instead of going south with King Richard, the French knights headed back to Jaffa, Acre, and Tyre. Therefore, Richard's forces were weakened. When Saladin saw what the Crusaders were doing, the sultan realized that Jerusalem was safe for the winter. He sent many of his soldiers home and reduced the forces defending the city.

During the early months of 1192, Richard's soldiers rebuilt the city of Ascalon. They constructed new walls to defend the city. Then it could serve the Crusaders as a major port on the Mediterranean. Richard tried to concentrate on the reconstruction of Ascalon. But he received troubling messages regarding his kingdom in England. During his absence in Palestine, Richard had left his homeland in the hands of his brother John. The king had directed that John should run the kingdom along with

William Longchamp, Richard's chancellor. Longchamp wrote the king that John did not intend to share power in England. Instead, John was acting like a king. He was calling himself the heir to Richard's throne. Richard had recently married Berengaria, who might produce a son. Therefore, John had no right to consider himself Richard's heir.

King Richard realized that he might need to return to England to defend his throne. Richard told his soldiers that he was planning to go home. With Richard unable to continue his leadership of the Third Crusade, his knights had to select a new leader. Some of them supported Guy of Lusignan. But many others believed that Guy lacked the military ability to lead knights in battle. After all, he had lost the Battle of Hattin. A majority of the Crusaders supported Conrad. He had saved the city of Tyre and participated in the siege of Acre. During the spring of 1192, Conrad was selected to become the new king of Jerusalem.

THE FINAL YEAR OF THE WAR

As a new campaigning season began in 1192, Saladin received another peace proposal from King Richard. Once again, Richard communicated this proposal through Saladin's brother, al-Adil. This time King Richard offered to split up the land in Palestine. Each side would agree to "keep what they now hold," and both Christians and Muslims would divide the city of Jerusalem."[4] While Saladin was considering this offer, Richard led his

THE DEATH OF CONRAD

Conrad never had an opportunity to take up his new position. In April, he was murdered in Tyre by two members of the Assassins. According to Muslim historian Imad ad-Din, the assassination occurred after King Conrad had finished dinner and gone outside:

> Suddenly two men fell upon him like two mangy wolves and their daggers stopped his movement and struck him down. . . . Then one of them fled and entered a church. . . . [Conrad], at death's door, but still with a flicker of life in him, said [to his own men who had run out to help him] 'Take me into the church,' and they took him in thinking that he was safe there. But when . . . one of the two murderers saw him, he fell on him to finish him off and struck him again, blow on blow. The Franks seized the two companions. . . .[5]

No one ever knew who had hired the assassins to commit the murder. Some Muslims believed that Richard had ordered the killing to remove Conrad. But there was also a rumor that Saladin had hired the Assassins to murder not only Conrad but also Richard.[6] With Conrad gone, Richard appointed a new king of Jerusalem. He knew that many people were opposed to Guy, so Richard chose his nephew, Henry of Champagne. (Richard instead made Guy the new king of Cyprus.) Henry had participated in the siege of Acre and accompanied Richard during the entire Crusade in Palestine. Henry married Isabella, who had been Conrad's wife. Together they planned to rule the Kingdom of Jerusalem once it was captured.

crusaders south from Ascalon in May. They attacked the Muslim fortress at Darum. This was a huge castle that guarded the entrance to Egypt. Richard moved up his catapults and began hurling huge rocks against the stone walls of Darum. Then his miners began to dig a tunnel underneath the walls and main gate. According to Baha al-Din, "they set fire to the mine," and the main gate fell crashing to the ground. "The defenders of the castle asked for a truce to enable them to consult the sultan, but the Franks allowed them no truce. They attacked even more strongly and took the place by force of arms."[7]

By this time, King Richard had decided to remain in Palestine. Problems still existed back in England. But the victory at Darum encouraged him to advance on Jerusalem. As Richard marched northward, Saladin prepared a defense of the city. At first, he planned to concentrate most of his troops inside Jerusalem. Among his generals were Mashtub and Saladin's son, al-Afdal. Many of the generals opposed Saladin's plan. As one of his advisors reported to him:

> The Mamlukes [sic] and the emirs as a body have met
> . . . and criticised . . . preparations for a siege. They
> said that this is not the best course and they fear
> that, when they are besieged, they will suffer what
> happened to those in Acre and then all the lands of
> Islam will be lost. The right plan is to meet in
> pitched battle. If God decrees that we defeat them,
> we will gain all their remaining territory.[8]

Saladin was worried about leaving Jerusalem open to attack. But he agreed with his generals and decided to follow their advice. Saladin left a small force in Jerusalem. Then he marched out of the city to prepare for a battle with the Crusaders. Meanwhile, King Richard had moved his army northward to Beit Nuba, northwest of Jerusalem. Skirmishes broke out between the Muslims and the Crusaders as they maneuvered for the decisive battle. Before this battle occurred, however, Richard briefly headed southward with a few of his knights. The king had been informed by a spy that a caravan of relief supplies was coming from Egypt to Saladin's army. As the caravan rested at night, Richard went into their camp. He was "disguised as an Arab. He saw them quietly resting, deep in sleep. He went back and called his men to horse. The surprise attack was close to dawn. He caught them unawares. . . ." Richard led a furious charge of his cavalry. Swinging his sword back and forth, he killed many of the Muslim enemy. Then he captured the entire caravan.[9]

JERUSALEM AND JAFFA

After this brief battle, King Richard returned to the main body of his army. Meanwhile, Saladin had sent some of his men out to poison all the wells on the road to Jerusalem. Richard realized that a march eastward from his camp would be extremely difficult. The hot summer months had already begun. Because of the poisoned wells, there was no water available along the march. The Crusader army might risk another disaster like Hattin if it tried to reach Jerusalem. Richard finally decided to turn back from his plan to attack the city.

During July, King Richard sent another peace proposal to Saladin. "It is not right for you to ruin all the Muslims, nor for me to ruin all the Franks," he said. This time Richard reduced his demands. He asked only for a single church inside Jerusalem. Saladin agreed to this request. He also agreed to Richard's proposal that Palestine should be divided between Muslims and Christians. But the sultan added one more provision. He wanted the Crusaders to destroy Ascalon. King Richard would not agree to give up such an important military position.[10]

When Saladin realized that the negotiations had broken down, he put his army on the march once again. King Richard had led his troops northward to the Muslim stronghold of Beirut. In July, Saladin decided to attack Jaffa. His army encamped outside the city and rolled up their catapults to begin knocking down the walls. The Christian defenders were under the command of Alberi of Rheims. They held out for a short period. But Saladin soon knocked down one of the gates to the city. Although the defenders tried to block the gate with shields, Muslim troops streamed over it. They then began going from house to house, stealing anything that they could find.

PAYING SALADIN'S TROOPS

Saladin's troops were paid in different ways. Some of his men were paid in cash each month. The higher ranking soldiers were paid with land grants. These were called *iqtas*.

124

Saladin was unable to stop the looting, which his soldiers felt was their right.

By early August, the defenders who still occupied part of Jaffa had decided to hand over the city. But by that time, they had received word that King Richard had called off his attack on Beirut. Richard was sailing down the Mediterranean toward Jaffa.

"As dawn approached," wrote a Muslim at the scene, "we heard the bray of Frankish trumpets and realized that a relief force had arrived." Saladin placed a small force on the shore to stop Richard from coming onto the beach. Inside Jaffa, the defenders had already started marching out to surrender. But after seeing Richard's ships, they went back into the city. Then the Crusaders began to attack the Muslims, driving them back toward the city gates. "They forced our soldiers out of the town. Our men were crowded together at the city gate with the result that many of them were close to meeting their doom," wrote Baha al-Din. At first, Richard did not come ashore. He did not know whether Jaffa had surrendered to Saladin. Then, one of the defenders inside the city saw Richard's galleys. He "leapt from the citadel to the habour side, which was sand and therefore did not injure him at all. He ran at full speed to the sea. A galley put in for him and took him to the king's galley, where he told his story."[11]

King Richard led his men ashore from the galleys. Wielding his sword, the king drove off the Muslim defenders. The rest of Saladin's forces began to retreat from Jaffa, which remained in the hands of the Crusaders. Saladin set up a new camp for his army outside the city.

But the siege could no longer continue successfully. The Crusaders could now supply Jaffa by sea with food and additional troops.

At this point, negotiations continued between King Richard and Saladin. Both men realized that their troops were tired of war and wanted peace. Yet they still disagreed about the future of Ascalon. Therefore, the negotiations were stalemated. Richard began to repair the damage done

Crusaders stormed ashore and forced Saladin's defenders out of Jaffa.

during the siege of Jaffa. To supervise the work, the king set up a small camp outside Jaffa. When Saladin heard about this, he made a daring plan to attack Richard's men at night. Saladin planned to capture the king, therefore winning a great victory over the Crusaders. Without their leader, they might retreat from Jaffa.

On August 4, Saladin and his soldiers traveled through the night. They wanted to storm Richard's camp the following dawn. But Richard and his troops had learned about the attack in advance. When it started, they put up a strong defense. Although some of Saladin's troops kept fighting, others began to retreat. Fighting on foot, after his horse was killed, King Richard tried to hold off the Muslims. As the battle continued, Saladin was told by one of his men that Richard did not have a horse to lead his troops. "That a King should be on foot with his men!" Saladin said. "It cannot be! Go. Take these two Arabian horses and lead them to him. Tell him that I send them to him, and that a man so great as he is should not be in parts such as these, on foot, with his men."

Historian James Reston called this decision by Saladin, "the crowning act of chivalry in the entire Third Crusade."[12] Richard eventually forced the Muslims to retreat, ending the battle. The Third Crusade had finally come to an end.

PEACE AND THE PASSING OF SALADIN

JAFFA WAS THE FINAL BATTLE OF THE THIRD Crusade. Saladin and Richard agreed to peace.

In August 1192, shortly after the Battle of Jaffa, King Richard came down with a serious illness and a high fever. Saladin sent him fresh fruit as well as ice from the mountain snows. Meanwhile, the sultan met with his emirs to plan another attack on Jaffa. With Richard ill, Saladin believed that the time had come to retake the city. But the emirs were opposed to another attack. They were exhausted from war. They told Saladin that the soldiers needed to return home to tend their fields and bring in their crops. They could not continue fighting against the Crusaders.

Meanwhile, negotiations between Richard and the Muslims began again. As in the past, King Richard negotiated directly with al-Adil. Much of the negotiation centered on Ascalon. Saladin still insisted that the Crusaders must give up the stronghold if they hoped to make peace. Finally, Richard agreed because he was too ill to continue fighting. He also wanted to return home to England.

The negotiators brought the word to Saladin, "The king has ceded Ascalon. . . . His purpose to make peace is sincere."[1] Saladin drew up a document that gave the cities along the Mediterranean coast to the Crusaders. These included Jaffa, Acre, Haifa, and Tyre. The Muslims retained control of the inland areas, including Jerusalem.

PEACE, AT LAST

When the peace agreement was taken back to Richard, he refused to sign. The king said that, after rebuilding Ascalon, he wanted to be paid for it. Richard was reminded by his advisors that he had agreed to destroy the city without any payment. His fever had apparently caused him to forget. "If I said it, I will not go back on it. Say to the sultan, 'Well and good! I accept these terms and look to your noble generosity.'" Although Richard was too weak to read the peace treaty, he extended his hand to the Muslim negotiators to indicate that he agreed with it. When Saladin received this news, he proclaimed it across Palestine. "Listen all! Peace has been arranged. Any person from their lands who wishes to enter ours may do so and any person from our lands who wishes to enter theirs may also do so."[2]

THE LONG JOURNEY OF RICHARD THE LIONHEART

King Richard left Palestine with a few of his followers and headed back to England. Meanwhile, in Europe, King Philip had once again turned against Richard. Philip believed that Richard had tried to outshine him in Palestine. The French king also wanted to conquer the lands that Richard controlled in France. Philip spread the word that Richard had planned the murder of Conrad of Montferrat. When Richard landed on the shores of the Adriatic, he narrowly escaped capture by one of Conrad's relatives—a local lord.

The king then headed northward into Austria, the kingdom of Leopold. Count Leopold had never forgiven the English King for not sharing the triumph at Acre in 1191. Richard was eventually surrounded by Leopold's soldiers at an inn. Leopold imprisoned Richard in a dreary castle along the Danube River. In England, John was pleased to hear that his brother had been captured. Hoping that Richard might never return to England, John soon expected to be king. At first, King Richard's whereabouts were unknown.

Richard's captors soon asked a huge ransom to release him. His mother, Eleanor of Aquitaine, succeeded in raising the ransom money. Richard was finally released early in 1194. He then returned to England.

Following the conclusion of peace, Saladin sent most of his army back to their homes. Muslim engineers were also sent to Ascalon to destroy the city's defenses. As the soldiers left, Saladin went to Jerusalem and began receiving Christian pilgrims. They wanted to visit the shrines that commemorated the life of Jesus Christ. The sultan held discussions with many of the pilgrims and invited them into his quarters to eat with him.

In the meantime, King Richard began to recover his health. In October, he left Palestine and began his long voyage home to England. About the same time, Saladin traveled from Jerusalem to Damascus. He held a family reunion with his brother al-Adil and his sons, al-Zahir and al-Afdal. Al-Zahir then left Damascus for Aleppo, where he served as governor. Before his son's departure, Saladin told him, "Beware of bloodshed. Trust not in that. Spilt blood never sleeps. . . . Win the hearts of your people . . . and of your emirs and ministers. Such position as I have was won by gentleness and conciliation."[3]

During the winter, Saladin and his brother al-Adil went hunting outside the walls of Damascus. By this time, Saladin was probably more than fifty-five, considered old during the Middle Ages. He had also lived strenuously. Saladin had conducted many military campaigns and lived on the battlefield during most of his adult life. By 1193, his health was declining, and he seemed very tired. Late in February, the sultan developed a high fever. Although Saladin briefly seemed to recover, his illness grew worse. On March 4, 1193, Saladin died.

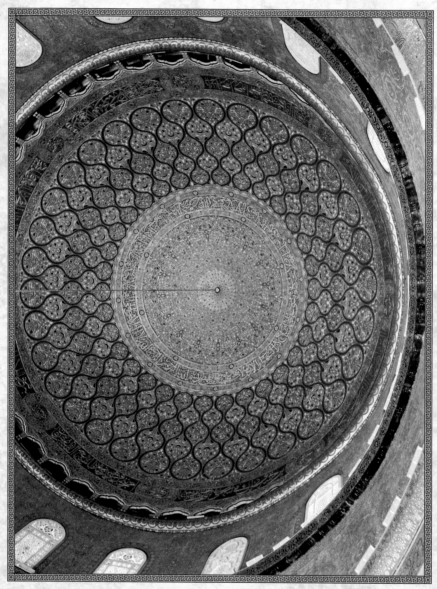

During his life, Saladin succeeded in protecting Jerusalem and the sacred Dome of the Rock from the Crusaders. The interior of the dome has beautiful golden decorations.

When his will was read, most of his subjects were amazed to discover that he left no money. The sultan owned no land or houses. In fact, he had set aside no money for his burial. Saladin had lived simply, devoting most of his life to building a Muslim empire and retaking Palestine from the Christians. In this, he was quite different from many of the European kings who surrounded themselves with riches and built great palaces.

Saladin's Legacy

AFTER HIS DEATH IN 1193, SALADIN'S REPUTATION grew, especially in Europe. He left behind him a legacy as a talented military leader with a reputation for great chivalry. In the Islamic world, Saladin was revered for uniting Muslims in a jihad to free Palestine from invaders. During the past century, modern Muslim leaders have tried to follow in Saladin's footsteps.

One of Saladin's greatest accomplishments was uniting the Muslims of Egypt and Syria. He then led them in a successful war to cast out the Crusaders from Palestine. Beginning in Egypt during the 1170s, Saladin had proven himself to be a skillful military and political leader. As wazir, Saladin recognized that he had little support among the Egyptian people. So he left Caliph al-Adid in place, although Saladin really ran Egypt. Once Caliph al-Adid died, Saladin took control of Egypt. He succeeded in ending the Fatimid Dynasty and making Sunni Islam the official religion of Egypt. He used force to put down an uprising by the Egyptian army. But he avoided a revolution among the Egyptian people. They did not rise up against Saladin and his soldiers, but accepted their rule. This was a tribute to Saladin's abilities as a strong, skillful, compassionate leader.

A SKILLED POLITICAL AND MILITARY LEADER

Saladin also strengthened Egypt's defenses against the Crusaders. He saw quite correctly that Egypt represented a valuable source of supply for his eventual takeover of Syria and his plans to conquer Palestine. Egypt produced rich wheat harvests that could be made into bread to feed his troops. In addition, the large Egyptian population could provide a steady stream of soldiers for Saladin's armies.

When Saladin advanced northward in 1174, he took Egyptian troops with him into Syria. Saladin was welcomed by many of the people in Damascus, the capital. This was due to his reputation as a successful general. But the Syrians also responded to his devout Muslim beliefs. Saladin tried to live by the teachings of the Koran. He also gained a reputation for fairness and openness to his people.

In the past, many Muslim leaders lived in lavish palaces, apart from the rest of the population. Saladin lived in simple surroundings. He was known for his humility and his generosity. His longtime friend, Baha al-Din, told a story about an old Mamluk who approached Saladin in his tent just before bedtime. The Mamluk had arrived with a request from one of the sultan's subjects. "I am tired

Saladin, sultan of Egypt and Syria

now," Saladin said and wanted to put off the matter until the next day. The Mamluk would not go away. So Saladin read the request and recognized that the person making it was a "worthy man." The Mamluk asked Saladin to put his signature on the request and grant the favor. "But there is no inkwell here," Saladin said, where he could dip his pen. "There is the inkstand at the back of the tent!" said the Mamluk. He did not expect that Saladin would arise and get the inkwell. "By Allah, you are right!" Saladin replied. Then he picked up the inkwell himself and signed the request. Other sultans would not have humbled themselves to listen to the Mamluk or to get the inkwell.[1]

Perhaps Saladin's greatest accomplishment was retaking Jerusalem from the Christians who had conquered it in 1099. This marked the high tide of Saladin's conquests. However, some historians believe that Saladin should have acted more aggressively after Jerusalem. They fault him for not taking the cities of Tyre, Tripoli, and Antioch.[2] From Tyre, the Crusaders marched on Acre, which fell after a long siege. King Richard I used Tyre and Acre as bases from which to reconquer part of Palestine.

King Richard has been praised for his own military skills that helped recapture part of Palestine. In July 1191, after the fall of Acre, he began a long march southward along the coast of Palestine. He kept his infantry on the inland side, protecting his cavalry from Muslim raiding parties. In addition, he kept in close touch with his ships, which supplied his troops. He held his troops together and refused to be drawn into a battle by Saladin's tactics.

In the past, the Muslims had sent their horse archers against the Christians, hoping to lure them out of formation. Once the Crusader cavalry charged, they would be ambushed by a larger force of Muslim horsemen. As historian Mark Abate wrote:

> Despite the numerical superiority of his army, he [Saladin] was unable to defeat Richard's forces in the field. Although Saladin had nearly every advantage, the best result he was able to achieve was a drawn-out stalemate that finally ended with a negotiated peace that revealed his military failures.[3]

Yet Saladin had accomplished enough. He had kept the Crusaders out of Jerusalem and reduced their power in Palestine. During the thirteenth century, new Crusades were mounted against Palestine. While the Muslims lost some of what Saladin had gained, they continued to hold Egypt and much of Palestine. Except for a short period in the thirteenth century, Muslims also retained control of Jerusalem.

SALADIN'S REPUTATION

Saladin's success in the Crusades has served as a model for later Muslim rulers. Among them was Colonel Gamal Abdal Nasser, who became president of Egypt in 1956. In 1958, President Nasser brought Egypt and Syria together in the United Arab Republic, much as Saladin had united them. Nasser compared himself to Saladin. In 1967, President Nasser launched an attack on Israel. The Israelis controlled much of the territory in Palestine that had once belonged to the Muslims during the Middle Ages. Unlike Saladin, however, President Nasser was not successful in regaining any of this land. Indeed, Israel won the war and expanded its own territory.

In 1970, President Nasser died. He was succeeded by his vice president, Anwar Sadat. In 1973, President Sadat launched another strike at Israeli forces. This war ended in a stalemate that eventually led to peace between Egypt and Israel. President Sadat traveled to Jerusalem, which was controlled by the Israelis, to initiate the peace process. For his efforts at making peace, Sadat was widely hailed among Western nations. "The comparison with Saladin is fruitful," wrote historian Karen Armstrong. "Until the twentieth century Saladin had actually been more widely revered in the West than he was in the East."[4]

The major reason Saladin had been praised was his willingness to make peace with the Crusaders. Europeans also revered Saladin because of his chivalry. The Middle Ages was a period of great cruelty. Military leaders, like Richard I and Saladin, thought nothing of executing captives. Richard killed the Muslims captured at Acre. Saladin executed the Templars and Hospitallers captured at the Battle of Hattin. Yet both men believed in a code of honor that was widely practiced by medieval knights. For example, oaths were taken seriously because they were sworn before God. Saladin had sworn to take Jerusalem by storm and kill the defenders. Therefore, after taking Jerusalem, he had to get permission to violate his oath so he could spare the Christian captives there.

Both Saladin and Richard fought fiercely against each other. But they also extended courtesies that would be unheard of today. When Richard lost his horse outside Jaffa in 1192, Saladin sent him a replacement. The sultan also sent Richard ice and fruit when he was suffering from a high fever. Saladin's chivalry appealed to Europeans, who believed in the same code of honor. As Karen Armstrong put it, "It is another example of the . . . grace with which Muslim and Christian could respond to one another in gestures that both perfectly understood."[5]

Historian Jonathon Phillips added,

> Western writers on the Third Crusade lauded his [Saladin's] generosity, his courteous treatment of women, his diplomatic skills and his military prowess. . . . In fact, Saladin occupied a central place in the most popular medieval "handbook" of chivalry—such was his fame that he had penetrated the very essence of Western knighthood! . . . In reality, Richard and Saladin were two of the greatest warriors and statesmen of the medieval age. They held each other in great respect, and both were unusual in attracting the admiration of their enemies. While Richard has a relatively low profile today, Saladin has become one of the major heroes of Islam.[6]

CHRONOLOGY

1055—Seljuk Turks conquer Baghdad.

1095—Pope Urban II calls the First Crusade.

1099—Crusaders capture Jerusalem and establish new states.

1138—Saladin is born.

1146—Second Crusade is launched.

1149—Crusaders fail to take Damascus, causing the Second Crusade to end.

1152—Saladin receives military training in Aleppo.

1162—Goes on campaign to Egypt.

1167—Returns to Egypt in second campaign.

1169—Becomes wazir of Egypt.

1171—Becomes sultan of Egypt.

1174—Is leader of Syria.

1176—Egypt and most of Syria under Saladin's control.

1185—Baldwin IV, king of Jerusalem, dies.

1187—Saladin wins victory over Crusaders at Hattin; captures Jerusalem and other Crusader cities; begins siege of the city of Tyre.

1188—Third Crusade is launched.

1189—Crusaders lay siege to Acre.

1190—German crusader, Frederick Barbarossa, dies; German crusading army crumbles.

1191—Acre surrenders to Crusaders, led by Richard I; Richard recaptures Crusader strongholds; Richard defeats Saladin at Battle of Arsuf.

1192—Crusaders fail to retake Jerusalem; Richard I and Saladin divide up Palestine; Richard returns to Europe.

1193—Saladin dies.

CHAPTER NOTES

CHAPTER 1. THE CONQUEST OF JERUSALEM

1. Karen Armstrong, *Holy War: The Crusades and Their Impact on Today's World* (New York: Random House, 2001), p. 257.

2. James Reston, Jr., *Warriors of God* (New York: Random House, 2001), p. 74.

3. "Some Medieval Accounts of Salah al-Din's Recovery of Jerusalem," 1988, <http://www.fordham.edu/halsall/med/salahdin.html> (August 14, 2006).

4. Francesco Gabrieli, *Arab Historians of the Crusades* (London: Routledge, 1969), pp. 141–142.

5. P. H. Newby, *Saladin in His Time* (London: Faber and Faber, 1983), pp. 120–121.

6. Armstrong, p. 260.

7. Gabrieli, p. 164.

8. Reston, p. 85.

9. "Letter of Pope Gregory VIII, *Medieval Sourcebook,* © 1997, <http://www.fordham.edu/halsall/source/hoveden1187.html> (August 14, 2006).

CHAPTER 2. SALADIN AND THE MUSLIM WORLD

1. Albert Hourani, *A History of the Arab Peoples* (Cambridge, Mass.: Harvard University Press, 1991), p. 33.

2. Ibid., p. 84.

3. Angus Konstam, *Historical Atlas of The Crusades* (New York: Facts on File, 2002), pp. 46–47.

4. Ibid., p. 75.

5. Amin Maalouf, *The Crusades Through Arab Eyes* (New York: Schocken Books, 1984), p. 144.

6. P. H. Newby, *Saladin in His Time* (London: Faber and Faber, 1983), p. 35.

7. Konstam, p. 109.

8. Andrew S. Ehrenkreutz, *Saladin* (Albany: State University of New York Press, 1972), p. 32.

CHAPTER 3. SALADIN IN EGYPT AND SYRIA

1. P. H. Newby, *Saladin in His Time* (London: Faber and Faber, 1983), p. 50.

2. Karen Armstrong, *Holy War: The Crusades and Their Impact on Today's World* (New York: Random House, 2001), pp. 236–237.

3. Francesco Gabrielli, *Arab Historians of the Crusades* (London: Routledge, 1969), pp. 89–90.

4. Newby, p. 56.

5. Andrew S. Ehrenkreutz, *Saladin* (Albany: State University of New York Press, 1972), p. 78.

6. Newby, p. 57.

7. Ehrenkreutz, p. 106.

8. Armstrong, p. 238.

9. Ibid., pp. 239–240.

10. Newby, p. 73.

11. Ibid., p. 74.

12. Ehrenkreutz, p. 162.

CHAPTER 4. THE CRUSADER KINGDOMS

1. Angus Konstam, *Historical Atlas of The Crusades* (New York: Facts on File, 2002), p. 80.

2. Joshua Prawer, *The World of the Crusaders* (New York: Quadrangle Books, 1972), pp. 73–74.

3. Ibid., p. 79.

4. Ibid., p. 72.

5. Alan Baker, *The Knight* (New York: Wiley, 2003), p. 42.

6. Konstam, p. 135.

7. Ibid., p. 148.

8. Baker, p. 170.

9. Medieval Sourcebook, "William of Tyre: The Foundation of the Order of Knights Templar," © 1997, <http://www.fordham.edu/halsall/source/tyre-templars.html> (August 14, 2006).

10. Prawer, p. 55.

11. Roger of Hoveden, "The Fall of Jerusalem, 1187," *Medieval Sourcebook,* © 1997, <http://www.fordham.edu/halsall/source/hoveden1187.html> (August 14, 2006).

Chapter 5. Saladin's Decisive Victory

1. Karen Armstrong, *Holy War: The Crusades and Their Impact on Today's World* (New York: Random House, 2001), p. 242.

2. James Reston, Jr., *Warriors of God* (New York: Random House, 2001), p. 19.

3. Ibid., p. 25.

4. David Nicolle and Angus McBride, *Saladin and the Saracens* (London: Osprey, 1996), p. 9.

5. Ibid., p. 12.

6. Reston, p. 38.

7. Ibid., p. 39.

8. Ibid., p. 42.

9. Ibn Shaddad Baha al-Din, *The Rare and Excellent History of Saladin*, trans. D. S. Richards (Ashgate: Aldershot, England, 2001), p. 28.

10. P. H. Newby, *Saladin in His Time* (London: Faber and Faber, 1983), p. 115.

11. Reston, p. 48.

12. Ibid., pp. 49–52.

13. Ernoul, "Battle of Hattin, 1187," n.d., <http://www.hillsdale.edu/personal/stewart/war/Med/Crusade/1187-Hattin.htm> (August 14, 2006).

14. Francesco Gabrieli, *Arab Historians of the Crusades* (London: Routledge, 1969), p. 121.

15. Newby, p. 118.

16. Reston, pp. 55–56.

17. Ibid., p. 57.

18. Gabrieli, pp. 137–138.

19. Ibid., pp. 178–179.

20. Ibid., p. 180.

Chapter 6. The Third Crusade

1. Malcolm Lyons and D.E.P. Jackson, *Saladin: The Politics of the Holy War* (New York: Cambridge University Press, 1997), p. 282.

2. *Saladin and Richard I of England: Was Saladin a Better Military Commander than Richard I?* n.d., <http://galenet.galegroup.com/servlet/History/hits?txt3=&txt2=&docNum=BT2306200366...> (December 31, 2005).

3. James Reston, Jr., *Warriors of God* (New York: Random House, 2001), pp. 123–134.

4. Francesco Gabrieli, *Arab Historians of the Crusades* (London: Routledge, 1969), p. 184.

5. P. H. Newby, *Saladin in His Time* (London: Faber and Faber, 1983), p. 137.

6. Gabrieli, p. 185.

7. Lyons and Jackson, p. 303.

8. Ibid.

9. Newby, p. 139.

10. Ibn Shaddad Baha al-Din, *The Rare and Excellent History of Saladin*, trans. D. S. Richards (Ashgate: Aldershot, England, 2001), pp. 110–111.

11. Ibid.

12. Ibid., pp. 147–148.

13. Reston, p. 158.

14. Gabrieli, pp. 201–202.

15. "The Saladin Tithe, 1188," © October 1998, *Medieval Sourcebook*, <http://www.fordham.edu/halsall/source/1188Saldtith.html> (August 14, 2006).

16. John T. Appleby, ed., *The Chronicle of Richard of Devizes of the Time of King Richard the First* (London: Thomas Nelson, 1963), p. 17.

17. Reston, pp. 129–130.

18. Angus Konstam, *Historical Atlas of The Crusades* (New York: Facts on File, 2002), p. 123.

CHAPTER 7. SALADIN AND RICHARD I

1. Ibn Shaddad Baha al-Din, *The Rare and Excellent History of Saladin*, trans. D. S. Richards (Ashgate: Aldershot, England, 2001), p. 150.

2. James Reston, Jr., *Warriors of God* (New York: Random House, 2001), p. 171.

3. John T. Appleby, ed., *The Chronicle of Richard of Devizes of the Time of King Richard the First* (London: Thomas Nelson, 1963), p. 44.

4. Reston, pp. 172, 175.

5. Malcolm Lyons and D.E.P. Jackson, *Saladin: The Politics of the Holy War* (New York: Cambridge University Press, 1997), p. 329.

6. Francesco Gabrieli, *Arab Historians of the Crusades* (London: Routledge, 1969), pp. 214–215.

7. Baha al-Din, p. 162.

8. Richard of Devizes, p. 44.

9. Baha al-Din, p. 165.

10. *Saladin and Richard I of England: Was Saladin a Better Military Commander than Richard I?* n.d., <http://galenet.galegroup.com/servlet/History/hits?txt3=&txt2=&docNum=BT2306200366...> (August 14, 2006).

11. Ibid., p. 170.

12. Ibid., p. 166.

13. Reston, p. 207.

14. "Battle of Arsuf," n.d., <http://myweb.tiscali.co.uk/sherwoodtimes/battleof.htm> (August 14, 2006).

15. Baha al-Din, p. 175.

16. Ibid.

17. Angus Konstam, *Historical Atlas of The Crusades* (New York: Facts on File, 2002), p. 145.

18. Reston, pp. 217–218.

19. Baha al-Din, pp. 178–179.

CHAPTER 8. BATTLE FOR A KINGDOM

1. Francesco Gabrieli, *Arab Historians of the Crusades* (London: Routledge, 1969), pp. 225–226.

2. Ibn Shaddad Baha al-Din, *The Rare and Excellent History of Saladin*, trans. D. S. Richards (Ashgate: Aldershot, England, 2001), p. 186.

3. Gabrieli, p. 230.

4. James Reston, Jr., *Warriors of God* (New York: Random House, 2001), p. 260.

5. Gabrieli, p. 239.

6. P. H. Newby, *Saladin in His Time* (London: Faber and Faber, 1983), p. 170.

7. Baha al-Din, p. 203.

8. Ibid., p. 210.

9. Ibid., p. 207.

10. Ibid., pp. 214–216.

11. Ibid., pp. 220–222.

12. Reston, p. 292.

CHAPTER 9. PEACE AND THE PASSING OF SALADIN

1. Ibn Shaddad Baha al-Din, *The Rare and Excellent History of Saladin,* trans. D. S. Richards (Ashgate: Aldershot, England, 2001), p. 228.

2. Ibid., pp. 229–231.

3. P. H. Newby, *Saladin in His Time* (London: Faber and Faber, 1983), p. 192.

CHAPTER 10. SALADIN'S LEGACY

1. Francesco Gabrieli, *Arab Historians of the Crusades* (London: Routledge, 1969), p. 106.

2. *Saladin and Richard I of England: Was Saladin a Better Military Commander than Richard I? n.d.,* <http://galenet.galegroup.com/servlet/History/hits?txt3=&txt2=&docNum=BT2306200366...> (December 31, 2005).

3. Ibid.

4. Karen Armstrong, *Holy War: The Crusades and Their Impact on Today's World* (New York: Random House, 2001), pp. 318–319.

5. Ibid., p. 271.

6. Jonathan Phillips, *Saladin, Richard the Lionheart and the Legacy of the Crusades,* n.d., <http://www.channel4.com/history/microsites/H/history/i-m/lionheart.html> (August 14, 2006).

Glossary

caliph—A successor to Muhammad.

emir—A local Muslim ruler.

feudalism—System of government used in Crusader states.

fief—Land given to knight who supported his lord.

hauberk—Coat of chain mail worn by a knight.

haute cour—High court, or council, of the king of Jerusalem.

Hijira—Muhammad's journey from Mecca to Medina.

jihad—Muslim holy war.

Koran—Muslim holy book containing Muhammad's words.

magonels—Giant catapults that hurled rocks.

Mamluks—Former Muslim slaves who fought in Saladin's army.

minarets—Towers on a mosque from which Muslims are called to prayer.

moat—Ditch, often filled with water, surrounding a castle.

mosque—Muslim religious center.

Outremer—The name for the Christian states in Palestine.

Shi'ites—A large Muslim sect.

sultan—A holder of power, or Muslim ruler.

Sunnis—A large Muslim sect.

wazir—Chief minister of the Muslim government.

FURTHER READING

Crompton, Samuel Willard. *The Third Crusade: Richard the Lionhearted vs. Saladin.* Philadelphia: Chelsea House Publishers, 2004.

Davenport, John. *Saladin.* Chelsea House Publishers, 2003.

Hancock, Lee. *Saladin and the Kingdom of Jerusalem: The Muslims Recapture the Holy Land in AD 1187.* New York: Rosen Publishing Group, 2004.

Hilliam, David. *Richard the Lionheart and the Third Crusade: The English King Confronts Saladin, AD 1191.* New York: Rosen Publishing Group, 2004.

Hilliam, Paul. *Islamic Weapons, Warfare, and Armies: Muslim Military Operations Against the Crusaders.* New York: Rosen Publishing Group, 2004.

Kavanaugh, Dorothy. *Islam, Christianity, and Judaism.* Broomhall, Pa.: Mason Crest Publishers, 2004.

Nicolle, David. *Historical Atlas of the Islamic World.* New York: Checkmark Books, 2003.

Stanley, Diane. *Saladin: Noble Prince of Islam.* New York: HarperCollins Publishers, 2002.

Internet Addresses

Battle of Hattin, 1187: Ernoul, a Frank.
<http://www.hillsdale.edu/personal/stewart/war/>
Click on "Medieval History" at the left. Select "Battle of Hattin, 1187" under "Crusades."

Medieval Sourcebook: Roger of Hoveden: The Fall of Jerusalem, 1187
<http://www.fordham.edu/halsall/source/hoveden1187.html>

Saladin and His Cairo
<http://touregypt.net/featurestories/saladin.htm>

INDEX